THE HEART OF THE REVOLUTION

THE HEART OF THE
REVOLUTION

The Buddha's Radical
Teachings on Forgiveness,
Compassion, and Kindness

NOAH LEVINE

HarperOne
An Imprint of HarperCollins*Publishers*

HarperOne

The teachings and quotes in this book have all come from the oral tradition of Buddhism. Noah learned these teachings from his teachers, as they did from theirs. The quotes have been handed down from generation to generation, all the way back to the Buddha.

HarperCollins website: http://www.harpercollins.com

HarperCollins®, ❦®, and HarperOne™ are
trademarks of HarperCollins Publishers

FIRST EDITION
Designed by Level C

Library of Congress Cataloging-in-Publication Data
is available upon request.

ISBN 978-0-06-171124-4

11 12 13 14 15   RRD (H)   10 9 8 7 6 5 4 3 2 1

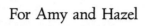

For Amy and Hazel

Contents

PART 1

FTW, OR AVOIDING THE DEAD END OF WORLDLINESS

PART 3

AVOIDING THE DEAD END OF RELIGION

Foreword

The *Heart of the Revolution* contains one of the most powerful and liberating messages in the world: wherever you are, your heart can be free. Nelson Mandela showed this when he walked with amazing dignity and compassion out of twenty-seven years of prison to become president of South Africa.

You too can free your heart. You need not be trapped by your past. Individually and collectively, our hearts can be released from the sufferings of our history. I have seen this over and over again on retreats, as meditators honorably face the pain of their history with courage, healing compassion, and forgiveness, and learn to move on. I have seen this in prisons and hospices and AA meetings, and among former victims and former combatants for peace in countries around the world.

The sufferings of our families and community and the world are built on lies—lies of fear and addiction, of racism, of trauma and hate. But they are not the end of the story. There is also a release from these lies.

When my teacher Maha Ghosananda, whose whole family was killed in the Cambodian genocide, gave teachings to twenty-five thousand traumatized survivors in their refugee camp, I wondered what he could say to those who had lost so much. He took his seat with dignity and chanted the Buddha's words over and over:

> Hatred never ceases by hatred
> But by love alone is healed.
> This is the ancient and eternal law.

Soon all twenty-five thousand refugees were chanting with him, faces covered in tears, giving voice to a truth even greater than their sorrows.

Forgiveness, compassion, and freedom to live your own life are available to you. These are your birthright. As Noah explains in these pages, "There is no one who is unable to love."

But how to do so? This is the real gift of this book. In it, Noah offers the Buddha's wise and systematic practices to quiet your mind and heal and liberate your heart.

Through these teachings, as you learn how to live wisely in the present and to liberate your fears of the past and future, you will develop confidence in the power of mindfulness. You will learn how to touch the struggles of your life with compassion, and develop faith that you can overcome confusion, self-hatred, and despair. You will learn the revolutionary freedom and happiness that come when you tell the truth and step out of deception, both your own and others.

And you will learn how to bring your clarity and compassion to a world that so desperately needs them.

This book is a gift to those who read its words.
Take them to heart, try them, and transform your life.
May you do so and be blessed.

Jack Kornfield

Spirit Rock Meditation Center

2011

Introduction

WELCOME TO THE REVOLUTION

The Buddha was a revolutionary, a radical advocate for personal and social transformation. He rejected the religious norms of his time and renounced all forms of greed, hatred, and delusion. He dedicated his life to going "against the stream," to the subversive path of an outlaw transient. He wasn't afraid to speak out against the ignorance in this world's political, social, and religious structures, but he did so from a place of love and kindness, from an enlightened compassion that extended to all living beings. The Buddha's teachings are not a philosophy or a religion; they are a call to action, an invitation to revolution.

I have always looked up to those who thought and lived outside the norms. Growing up, I had a sense that there was something very wrong with this world. Punk rock pointed out to me that many of the norms and laws of this land were constructs of a puritanical and corrupt religious nation. Until I found the practices and teachings of the Buddha, I was stuck in the conundrum of seeing some of the problems but having no solution.

I have had a lifelong fascination with outlaw culture. When I was a kid, bikers, Black Panthers, lowriders, gangsters, and punx were my heroes. Outlaw bikers wear a patch on their jackets that has "1%" printed within a diamond shape. That emblem signifies that they—the "1%ers"—stand apart from law-abiding citizens. The tradition originated in the 1950s as a result of the famous 1947 biker riot in Hollister, California, which was later dramatized in the movie *The Wild One* with Marlon Brando. Reporting on the riot, a journalist trying to defend the masses of motorcycle enthusiasts wrote a story about how 99 percent of the people in this world who ride motorcycles are law-abiding citizens. He said that it is only the remaining 1 percent who give the rest a bad name, living outside the law. Of course, the outlaw bikers took this as a compliment and ran with it. They rebelled against the mindless, mainstream conventionality of the fifties and were proud of it.

The Buddha is reported to have said that he thought "only a handful of people in each generation"—the spiritual 1%ers—would be willing to do the hard work of training the heart and mind through meditation, ethical behavior, and unconditional love for all sentient beings. His message was radical. Like the outlaw bikers of the fifties, he bucked the conventions and norms of his day. His practice was hard, but the insights and happiness it promised were new and potentially world-shattering.

With 6.8 billion people in this world, "only a handful" could very easily mean somewhere around 1 percent, or 68 million people. Do you suppose there are 68 million people in this world who are walking a spiritual path with heart? I don't know. But what I do know is that it is rare for Buddhists, Christians, Jews, Muslims, Hindus, atheists, agnostics, scientists, or whatever to be open-hearted, to be free from ill will, resentment, and ignorance. It makes sense that the path of love and compassion, of kindness and appreciation, is tread only by the 1 percent of this world who have had the good fortune to find the willingness to reject the false teachings of religion and have turned inward to find the truth for themselves.

When I first heard the radical Buddhist teachings on loving-kindness, compassion, and forgiveness, I was incredibly skeptical. Coming from a background of drugs and violence, I saw those heart-qualities as undesirable and perhaps even unsafe. In the circles I ran in, compassion was seen as equivalent to weakness and would make you vulnerable to harm and abuse. I learned early on that this world was full of pain and seemed to lack much kindness. In reaction to the pain in my life, I began to close my heart and to harden myself against all forms of love. So it was with great hesitance that I experimented with Buddhist practices of kindness and compassion. In the beginning I don't think forgiveness was even in my vocabulary. The only reason I opened myself to these meditation practices, often called *heart practices,* at all was because I had tremendous faith in the practice of mindfulness (paying attention to the present moment), in the Buddha, and in my teachers, who assured me that it was safe to love again.

As I looked into these heart practices, I heard things like "Love is your true nature" and "The heart has a natural tendency toward compassion." Now, I had already been meditating for some time, examining my inner world through mindfulness, and I didn't see any of the love and compassion of which these teachers spoke. When I looked into my heart and mind, I saw only fear, anger, hatred, judgment, more fear, and a lot of lustful cravings. When I sat quietly, paying attention to my breath, my attention was repeatedly drawn into fantasies of vengeful destruction or pornographic sex. One moment I was bashing in my stepfather's head with a Louisville Slugger; the next I was in a threesome with Madonna and Traci Lords. I was pretty sure that such sludge was all that was in there. Mindfulness helped me deal with my inner confusion—it allowed me to ignore my mind at times and not take it so personally at others—but it didn't seem to be magically creating a loving heart out of my inner critic/terrorist/pervert/tough guy.

In the early days of my meditation practice I was interested only in mindfulness. I had been introduced to various breath awareness meditations, and as a result I experienced the direct benefits of concentration and mindfulness. I immediately found temporary relief from fear of the future and shame about the past. Learning to train my mind to pay close attention to the present moment was difficult, but fruitful. I experienced immediate, if only momentary, relief from the suffering I continuously created with my mind's tendency to be lost in the future and past. Before I began my meditation practice, whenever my mind started to worry about what would happen in the future I would get completely sucked into the fears and often become convinced that the worst-case scenario would play out. Mindfulness gave me the tools to let go of those thoughts and to bring my attention into the body's experience of the breath. Mindfulness made sense to me, and it wasn't difficult to gain a verified faith in that aspect of Buddhism. For me, mindfulness proved to be the doorway to the rest of the Buddha's Dharma, or teachings. I came to believe that it was going to be possible to train my mind, but I still had no hope for my heart.

When I did practice loving-kindness meditations (I'll walk you through several in the course of this book), my mind was so critical and resistant that my efforts seemed to make my mind louder and my heart harder rather than softer. But I continued to practice loving-kindness meditations anyway. Again, the fact that I had seen that mindfulness worked gave me some confidence to try the rest of the Buddha's teachings. Besides, what did I have to lose? I was already unhappy. My heart was already hard. Gradually I began to see that underneath my fears and lusts was a genuine desire to be free from suffering. Mindfulness had given me my first taste of that freedom, and I wanted more.

So, without much hope, I eventually committed to including kindness, compassion, and forgiveness meditations in my daily practice. It was a slow and difficult process to learn to love myself and others. Eventually, though, I began to understand what the Buddha and my teachers had been talking about; I began to get glimpses of genuine kindness and compassion and to experience moments of forgiveness. But I have to admit that it took years.

Over my years of meditation practice, which has included regular periods of silent intensive retreats, ranging from five days to three months in length, I have gradually come to experience the compassion, forgiveness, mercy, kindness, and generosity that the Buddha promised would be found. My heart has softened; my mind has quieted down. These days, I rarely want to bash anyone's head in. When I think of my stepfather, I do so with compassion for how much suffering he must have been in to have been such a jerk back then. My mind focuses easily on the task at hand, and I often feel warmth and kindness toward all beings. I now know that compassion is a natural quality of my heart—one that was lying dormant, waiting to be uncovered.

The Buddhist path is a process of discovery, recovery, and a gradual uncovering of a loving heart. I see the process of awakening and healing as being like the activity at an archaeological dig. In the early days I worked just on the surface. Mindfulness was a tremendous relief, and it acted like a metal detector that allowed me to know there were precious treasures beneath the ground. Mindfulness was also the shovel that began the excavation. But as I started to dig, I first found all the layers of sediment that were covering the heart. The heart practices allowed for a further refining of the soil. I was beginning to sift through the rubble, hoping to immediately find treasure. The unsettled feeling I got during my early days of compassion and kindness exercises came about because I was uncovering all the skeletons that had been buried over the years of trying to avoid the pains of my childhood and adolescence. I had become quite skilled, in my early years, at covering the insecurity and reactivity. But each meditative effort of forgiveness, kindness, or compassion removed another shovelful of dirt, each one getting me closer to the forgotten truth of my heart.

At times, the heart practices serve as even finer instruments of archaeology—that is, as brushes used to gently sweep away the remaining dust covering the treasures of the heart. Meditations are versatile in that way: sometimes you need a shovel to do the heavy lifting, and at other times you need something gentler, very subtle and refined, just to dust off the heart, as it were. But as we know, sometimes uncovering an ancient city can take a lifetime. There is no timetable that we can count on. There is no guarantee that we will reach the forgotten treasure of compassion anytime soon. What is promised is that it is there, waiting, and at times we can hear it calling to us, begging to be uncovered. The path of meditative training, if followed correctly and with persistence, will always lead to the recovery of our lost love and compassion, one scoop at a time.

I can say all this with confidence, because I have experienced it directly, as you will. These days, my life is filled with a general sense of trust and friendliness. My relationships with my parents, my friends, and my wife and daughter are sourced from appreciation, love, compassion, and forgiveness. But perhaps more important is the attitude of loving-kindness that permeates my attitude toward strangers. I spent my early life at war with the world. The heart practices of the Buddha taught me to surrender, but not to give up the commitment to creating a positive change. What was once a rebellion fueled by hatred is now a revolution fueled by compassion.

Now, I feel that it is only fair to also offer a warning: the path to uncovering our heart's positive qualities is a radical one, fraught with the demons of the heart/mind that in Buddhism we call *Mara*. Mara is the aspect of heart/mind that creates roadblocks, gives excuses, procrastinates, and urges us to avoid all the unpleasant mind-states that accompany the healing of awakening. Mara is the inner experience of all forms of greed, hatred, and delusion. Mara—often personified as an opponent—will attack with vengeance at times, for by committing to the heart's liberation, we are committing to facing Mara directly. The Buddha spoke of his battle with Mara, and noted that victory over Mara was won with the weapons of love, compassion, equanimity, and appreciation. After the Buddha's initial victory, Mara did not give up, however. Mara continued to live with the Buddha throughout his whole life. The Buddha was constantly vigilant, always meeting Mara with a loving awareness, always disarming him with the heart's wisest responses.

There is no one who is unable to love, forgive, or be compassionate. Ability is our birthright. All that is required is the desire and willingness to take on those challenges. Most people would confess the desire to be free from the hatred, anger, and fear that they live with. There are some, though, who have been so badly injured and confused that they have lost all hope or have created a belief in hatred as a noble and necessary quality. It seems as if this is the case in many of the Western religions: when you worship a God who is judgmental, wrathful, and vengeful, it makes sense that those same qualities would become acceptable and perhaps even desirable in you.

But before I go off on my atheist Buddhist rant, let me say that although it seems that true love and the willingness to uncover the heart-qualities of forgiveness, mercy, and compassion are rare, Buddhists are not the only ones who are using those practices. As a matter of fact, I think that very few Buddhists are actually applying the teachings of the Buddha to their heart/mind. The Buddha spoke of a *middle path,* a path that leads "against the stream" and between two dead ends. The first dead end is that of worldliness, or seeking happiness from material or sensual experiences. The second dead end is that of religion, or seeking happiness from devotion and belief in external salvation. I think that most Buddhists have fallen into the dead end of religion. Be careful that you do not make the same mistake.

I hope that this view does not discourage you, but rather that it inspires you to make sure that you're part of the rare and precious revolutionaries of heart, of the compassionate 1%ers. Acknowledging that only a handful in each generation will do what needs to be done does not have to be bad news. Actually, it is great news; it is real and realistic. That *anyone* can find the willingness and courage to follow this difficult path is a great victory for humanity. And remember: 1 percent is millions and millions of people!

I welcome you to the revolution as a comrade in heart. If you follow this path, you will free yourself from all of the unnecessary suffering of life and you will inspire others to do the same. The practices in this book are not a quick fix; they are a map to a hidden treasure. You will have to do all of the digging yourself. Although this work is best done with the support of teachers and a community of fellow archaeologists, ultimately you will have to do all the heavy lifting—or letting go, as it may be. Your life will be transformed, as mine has been, and together we will be among the 1%ers who create a positive change in this world.

Part 1

FTW, OR AVOIDING THE DEAD END OF WORLDLINESS

Chapter 1

WIDE AWAKE

don't sleep on reality; it's time to
wipe the dust from our eyes

Here we are, human beings, living with the consequences of having been born. I assume that most of you know the basic truths of existence, but I would like to offer an overview anyway, as a reminder to some and as a revelation to others.

We are born into a mind/body/heart process ruled by a psychological/biological/emotional survival instinct that is out of harmony with reality. The normal condition of human beings is a sleeplike state of nonwisdom. The evolutionary process of human beings is dictated by a natural desire to live and to pursue happiness. But our survival instinct, which is controlled by the mind/body, keeps alive an unrealistic hope for a life that is always pleasurable and never painful. Our bodies naturally crave pleasure, which we think equals happiness, safety, and survival. Conversely, we hate pain, which we think equals unhappiness and death. We are constantly ruled by this survival instinct, meeting each pain with aversion and each pleasure with attachment. Does this sound familiar so far?

The problems here are numerous. Our natural lust for pleasure and hatred of pain help us survive for as long as circumstances and the body's impermanence allow. In that sense we are dependent on our base cravings to survive. They are not the enemy; they are a necessary function of life. But that's *all* they are: as we know all too well, a life lived chasing pleasure and running from pain leads only to more and more suffering and confusion. Our survival instinct does not grant us happiness, only temporary survival. A life based on craving and aversion is a miserable existence at best; at times it becomes downright unbearable.

Instinct Versus Impermanence

The reason that our survival instinct sometimes leads us into misery is that it runs up against the truth of impermanence. We are born into a mind/body process that is constantly changing and a world that is constantly changing. *Everything* is impermanent—every pleasure, every pain, every body. But our survival instinct craves permanence and control. The body wants pleasure to stay forever and pain to go away forever. This is the very cause of attachment and aversion. The fact of impermanence leads to a generalized dissatisfaction. We are constantly struggling with loss: grieving the cessation of each experience and trying in vain to create stability out of transience. And yet happiness and stability are not our birthright. Loss and grief come as *unavoidable consequences* of birth.

When we attach to impermanent objects—sensations, thoughts, feelings, people, places, things—we are always left with the stress and grief of loss, because everything around us is always changing; it is always being pulled beyond our reach. Our grasping, our fighting against impermanence, results in loss and the suffering that comes with trying to hold on to the constantly changing reality. It's rather like trying to play tug-of-war with a much stronger opponent: when we begin to lose, as we always will, we can choose to let go or to hold on and receive the "rope burns" of attachment. The survival instinct tells us to hold on; the Buddha urges us to let go.

Our survival instinct gives us bad advice not just with attachment but also with aversion. When we meet unpleasant experiences with aversion, as our instinct tells us to do, we are causing them to last longer than they need to. All unpleasant thoughts, feelings, and sensations are impermanent; trying to push them away is futile and results in stress, anger, and suffering. It's as if with our aversion we created a dam in the flow of experience. Rather than letting impermanence do its job, we block the passing of the pain. We do this in a variety of ways—through suppression, avoidance, ignoring, self-medicating, or hardening the heart and closing down to life. Again, as a survival instinct aversion is *necessary*—we have to hate pain to survive—but it doesn't leave us with much freedom or happiness. When it comes to aversion, the survival-based life is a life of fear and loathing. Our instincts tell us to hate pain and try to get rid of it; the Buddha urges us to meet pain with mercy and compassion.

Now, I am not suggesting that we just accept every painful experience that life presents us or that we should never try to avoid pain or seek pleasure. Not at all. What I'm saying is that there is a lot of unpleasantness in life that is simply unavoidable. Our instinct fails to acknowledge that fact and tries to avoid *all* unpleasantness. That is impossible, but by all means avoid what you can. Likewise, enjoy pleasure as often as it is appropriate. As we practice meditation and live an ethical life, it will become more and more clear when it is time to accept the pains or enjoy the pleasures and when it is wise to refrain or avoid. The Buddha teaches us that it is possible to live a balanced life—that is, a life that enjoys pleasure without clinging to it and that meets unavoidable pain with tenderness and care. I call this *nonattached appreciation* and *compassionate response-ability*. I will go into detail about how to develop these skills in subsequent chapters.

We can all concede, at the thought level, that everything is impermanent; there is always going to be some level of difficulty and dissatisfaction in life. However, the mind/body tends to take this all very personally. This is because the evolved human condition has resulted in a brain that creates a *self*. The sense of being a permanent, fixed identity—a self—is a construction of the mind/body. Each one of us is a constantly evolving and unfolding *process,* not a fixed identity. This aspect of reality—that is, our own changing nature—seems to be at odds with the human survival instinct, so the mind creates a fixed identity that takes everything personally and clings to the notion of "I," "me," and "mine." But this solution is based on ignorance and a lack of investigation. Believing in a permanent self is like believing in a permanent rainbow. We all know that rainbows are temporary optical illusions based on the factors of sunlight, moisture, and heat. The environment creates each rainbow like the mind creates a self. Both creations are relatively real, in that we can genuinely experience them temporarily; but just as the factors that created the illusion (whether rainbow or self) arose, so will they also pass. There is no permanent self; there is no permanent rainbow. It is not true to say that there is *no* self at all or that *everything* is empty or illusory, but it *is* true that everything is constantly changing and that there is no solid, permanent, unchanging self within the process that is life. Everything and everyone is an unfolding process. Meditation can help us see that more fluid aspect of being.

Those of us who seek guidance through the practices of Buddhism are not trying to escape the human condition or the pleasures and pains of the human mind/body. Our job is to live an embodied and fully human life. What the meditative life offers—what the Buddha encourages—is a path to transforming our relationship to ourselves and the world.

Mindfulness is one of the keys. By bringing wise attention to the present-time experiences of being, we begin to respond more skillfully to each moment. We begin to see that resistance is futile and that our only hope is to respond to the truth of life with greater acceptance and compassion. The Buddha offers us a very practical guide for being wise and compassionate people. He teaches a humanistic psychosocial shift in consciousness and action. We are asked to embrace life as it is and to respond wisely to the reality we encounter. Buddhism should never be seen as an escapist or life-denying approach to living. It is simply a *better* way to live—a way that maximizes happiness and minimizes suffering.

The Piles

Let me offer another, more detailed explanation of what's happening here. The path of freedom is a gradual loosening of the misidentifications that create our suffering. The Buddha referred to the process as being like the fraying of a tightly wound rope: little by little the rope begins to fray and come apart. These misidentifications are traditionally referred to as the *skandhas*— "heaps" or "piles"—in Buddhism. The piles result in five different aspects of life that we tend to cling to as our fixed identity or misidentity: the body itself, the sense impression or feeling tones of the body, the mind or objects of the thinking mind (which include thoughts and the roots of emotions), perception (which includes memory), and consciousness.

As long as we hold to the incorrect view that any of these processes of the mind or body comprises who we ultimately are, we are chained to the causes and conditions that give rise to suffering. Taking any of these experiences as who we are at our core is inevitably going to be a cause of suffering. Why? Because of the uncontrollable and unreliable nature of these piles of life. When we believe that we are our bodies, we inevitably feel betrayed by the natural processes of sickness, old age, and death. When we believe that we are our minds, we suffer the fate of almost constant judgment, comparison, and fear. Freedom comes from the meditative disciplines that allow us to see clearly the impermanent, impersonal, and unsatisfactory nature of these five factors of existence.

Let's examine the piles one by one:

1. The Body

The human body is a process involving the four elements. Only earth, air, water, and heat are present in the human form. These four elements make up *all* of creation, both internally and externally. As the body is created in the womb, it is the four elements of the mother's body that create the fetal form. As the body is born into the world, the earth elements, mixed with water, air, and heat, create the sustenance that allows survival and growth. By absorbing the four elements, each body matures and converts these elements into flesh and blood.

All of the physical life in a body is a process of ceaseless change. From childhood onward our bodies are constantly changing, growing, maturing, and then eventually beginning to decay. The physical body arises out of the four elements and at death returns to the four elements. Throughout our life in the body, we become more and more identified with our physical form. We rarely question the organic process that is unfolding, and we rarely pause to acknowledge the impermanent quality of the body. We remember being children and we know that our bodies have changed over the years, but it rarely occurs to us that there is not one cell remaining in our body from childhood. The physical matter of the child's body is completely gone; only a memory remains. Every cell has been replaced by new cells. But the mind creates a delusion that this is the same body.

Thus we become the pile of suffering that is the impermanent body. This body is demanding and fragile; it is subject to sickness, old age, and death; it gives rise to the craving for more pleasure and less pain. Freedom from misidentification with the body does not come from self-denial and destruction of the physical form; rather, it comes from a radical shift in our understanding of what it means to be alive.

The Buddhist path of mindfulness meditation begins with a deep investigation of the body and its functions. Through meditative wisdom we come to understand that we are the temporary caretakers of the body, living with all of the phenomena of a nervous system, a digestive tract, an involuntary cardiopulmonary system, and so on. The body is not who we are; it is just what we are currently experiencing. Freedom from being the pile of the body is often the first step in the process of liberation that is called *enlightenment* or *awakening*. Of course, as with all other insights, breaking the misidentification with the body can take place only moment to moment. It is unlikely that we read these words, reflect on the truths exposed here, and then never again fall into the wrong view of belief that the body is who we are. It is more likely that over years and years of meditative practice we slowly loosen the identification and gradually awaken to the freedom of knowing that we have a body, recognizing that it is not our permanent or fixed identity. This is often the first aspect of the fraying of the rope of misidentification.

2. Sense Impressions

Life in the body is constantly accompanied by pleasant, unpleasant, or neutral sense impressions. Our mind/body process is wired to experience all things as either pleasurable, unpleasant, or neither. As noted earlier, a built-in survival mechanism causes us to prefer the pleasant experiences over the unpleasant ones and to ignore or find boring the times of neutrality. This is where the pile of sense impressions comes in. We mistakenly bind ourselves to being content only when life is feeling pleasurable. We become so identified with the sense impressions of the body that when the body is experiencing unpleasant phenomena, we create suffering on top of the pain, thus staying in the cycle of obeying the dictates of the body's preference for pleasure.

The next step in the process of liberation is to break this chain reaction of suffering whenever life is unpleasant and feeling content only when life is pleasurable. The second level of Buddhist insight meditation, then, is an in-depth investigation of the sense impressions within the body. Through moment-to-moment mindfulness we come to see the impermanent, impersonal, and unsatisfactory nature of both pleasure and pain. It is all constantly changing, nothing staying as is long enough to get attached to. Freedom comes when we learn to accept what is and break our vain attempts to control the uncontrollable. This is easier said than done, of course. We are being asked here to do something that is counterinstinctual. As I said earlier, identification with the sense impressions is a built-in survival instinct. The body will always crave pleasure and hate pain; that's what bodies are predisposed to do. Liberation comes from the radical shift in awareness that no longer identifies with the body's cravings and therefore has the free will to respond with compassion to pain and with nonclinging to pleasure. This is the freedom from the second pile of suffering.

3. Thoughts and Emotions

The mind's objects—our thoughts and emotions—are the next experience that we mistakenly identify with, and this misidentification contributes to confusion and unhappiness. Part of our human experience is the ability to think and to experience emotions. The objects of the thinking mind are an integral part of life. After all, we need to be able to plan and remember, to create and analyze. The mind is not a problem in and of itself. Actually, it is a necessity and can be an ally in overcoming the causes of suffering. But the mind also has a mind of its own, as it were, and tends to run on old and often outdated software.

There are two kinds of thoughts: intentional and unintentional—in other words, those of our deliberate creation and those that are mind-created, or nonvolitional. When I say "the mind has a mind of its own," I am referring to nonvolitional thoughts that arise without our intention or permission. As with the body's sense impressions, the human tendency is to take whatever arises in the mind personally. We become identified with our thoughts; believing every thought that arises in our mind, we become attached to our thinking process and feel that mind objects are who we are. For instance, when we're driving down the road and someone cuts us off in traffic, the core experience is fear: our survival instinct kicks in, creating an unintentional reaction. But the fear is usually covered by the experience of anger, which the mind creates (likewise unintentionally). We tend to take the mind so personally that we then spend time being angry: "I am pissed off at that bad driver." The truth is: fear arose, then anger arose, and both will pass if we let them. But our lack of understanding that fear and anger are impersonal survival instincts of the mind and body can ruin our whole day. We become an angry pile!

From a Buddhist perspective the mind is just another organic process of the body. Yes, we can think, and yes, the mind offers views and opinions based on past experiences, but the whole process is more impersonal and universal than we know. The mind becomes a hindrance when we mistake the contents of the thinking mind for our true identity. Much of what arises in the mind is just programmed by our survival instinct: "How can I get more pleasure?" "How can I avoid pain?" This is the crux of what the mind is usually doing. If we believe every thought or feeling that arises in the mind, we stay chained to suffering like a slave to his master. It is not the mind that is the problem; it is our lack of understanding that the mind is conditioned to deal with craving and aversion in particular ways. The mind is not who we *are*. It is just another aspect of living in a human body.

The mind experiences both thoughts and emotions. Emotions arise first in the mind and then are experienced in the body, and they are accompanied by a "feeling tone" of being pleasant or unpleasant. If we are paying attention, we can see the mind/body connection here: this pile of experience is connected to the first two. It is not the thought or emotion that causes suffering; it is our attachments and aversions, our lame attempts to control pleasure and pain, which cause suffering.

We break the chains of suffering by breaking our "addiction" to the mind. As with any other addiction, the difference between an addict of the mind and a nonaddict is that a nonaddict can take thoughts or leave them, depending on what is appropriate at the time. Most of us have very little ability *not* to take on the mind's views and opinions. We walk around strung out on our own thought processes, believing whatever arises in the mind. We therefore stay identified with the pile of confusion and cravings that fuel most thoughts and feelings. Perhaps it should not be "I think; therefore I am" but rather "I think I am my mind; therefore I suffer."

Again, it is only through a deep meditative transformation that we can escape the bondage of the mind. We cannot think our way to freedom; we must retrain the mind to see through its own ignorant tendencies.

4. Perception

The next step on the path of freeing ourselves from being identified with these piles is a radical transformation in how we relate to perception. Our perceived experience is flawed, because we see through the lenses of conditioned craving and aversion. Our mind holds on to resentments in a vain attempt to protect us from future harm. We begin to perceive a solid, separate existence where there is none—the self that I mentioned earlier, which we create based on memory. The pile of perception also leads us to deny impermanence: we *perceive* things as permanent, and thus we *assume* them to be permanent. There can be no freedom from suffering as long as we continue to perceive ourselves as separate, autonomous beings and our conditions as permanent. The perception of self as separate from others begins to break down when we see, through meditative reflection, the universal and interdependent nature of all things.

The mind is confused; it naturally creates a sense of separation and individuality. But this is a misperception. Although we may *feel* separate, it is only because a lack of true wisdom and understanding is blocking the truth of universal connectedness. The more we understand impermanence, the more we understand that on a subtle, perhaps even atomic level, we are just an unfolding pile of energy.

5. Consciousness

Consciousness, which receives all of the phenomena of mind and body that we have thus far been investigating, may prove to be the most challenging misidentification to break. Many wise beings have settled for an explanation of existence that rests on the misperception that we are the consciousness in which all of the world is arising. From a Buddhist perspective, consciousness is just another impersonal, impermanent, and unsatisfactory aspect of existence. Consciousness is not self; it is not our true nature. Rather, it is just another phenomenon of mind. Consciousness receives the mind's and body's sense impressions, receives our emotions and perceptions, but ultimately there is no owner of the consciousness; on the contrary, consciousness experiences itself. We are thoughts without a thinker, sensations without a sensor, perceptions without a perceiver. The mind and body are experiencing themselves. Stop taking it all so personally; stop falling into the pile of consciousness as self. This is the final task of liberation.

As my friend Eric likes to say, "Don't be such a pile."

Karma

As we try to let go of the grasping and aversion that our survival instinct urges on us, and seek instead to accept the impermanent, impersonal, and unsatisfactory nature of life, we are guided by the law of karma. We live on a plane of existence that has many natural and irrefutable laws. Some of these we are all familiar with, such as gravity and the concept that energy is neither created nor destroyed. The law of karma—all intentional actions have consequences—is equally irrefutable. It means, in essence, that we are totally and completely responsible for all of our intentional actions and the consequences that each action creates. In short, no one gets away with anything, ever.

For example, if you tell a lie but don't get caught, you will still pay. The karmic consequence of that action will usually be a feeling of guilt or fear of being found out. In the long run, those who practice dishonesty begin to live a dual life, feeling disconnected from themselves. They no longer have the ability to experience true happiness, because the law of karma makes true happiness dependent on truthfulness.

Here we are, alive, at least temporarily, on a planet and in a human condition that is out of whack with the reality it inhabits. The challenges we face are immense but not insurmountable. The Buddha has left us a detailed map of the terrain we have to navigate, a way forward that encourages us to wade into the stream and travel against the torrents of greed, hatred, and delusion. The outcome of the practices of Buddhist meditation is to open our eyes, allowing us to be wide awake. We must be careful not to ensnare ourselves in the trap of seeking happiness from the world—in fact, FTW. The world cannot supply genuine security or true happiness. We must also be careful not to become overzealous in our spiritual aspirations and thus fall into the trap of religion. The meditative practices that are offered in this book are not meant to inspire religious devotion or offer a quick fix; rather, they will help build a long-term engagement with our own heart, allowing us to uncover what has always been there.

Chapter 2

TRAINING THE MONKEY

the path of practice for the wild at heart

At the center of our human experience is the emotional complexity that we call "heart." Our hearts have the capacity for great love and deep joy, but also the capacity for unthinkable cruelty and hatred. Of course the heart that we are talking about is not the cardiac muscle that resides in the chest. But interestingly enough, when asked to locate their emotional heart or the center of their emotional being, most people point to a place in the center of the chest, the solar plexus, which is very close to where the physical heart lives. Indeed, what happens in the emotional heart often has an effect on the physical heart. For instance, romantic love can increase a person's heart rate, while grief can create a feeling of constriction around the cardiac muscle.

Despite these physical reactions, we know, through mindfulness and Buddhist psychology, that the mind is where emotions arise first. Without introspective investigation it may seem as if emotions are arising in the body first—fear, for example, is initially felt as a physical rush of adrenaline. It is the body's total and complex interconnection with the mind that creates this illusion. What you will find, if you pay close attention, is that emotions arise first as mental objects and are then almost instantly experienced as physical phenomena. In fact, the Buddha encouraged both mind and heart training, and at times in his teaching he used the word *citta*, which has the dual meaning of both heart and mind. The Buddha understood that our minds are not separate from our hearts; on the contrary, our hearts are completely connected to what is happening in our minds. Please keep all of this in mind (so to speak) as I use terms such as *heart* and *mind* throughout the book. They are often—but not always—interchangeable; and I often combine them into heart/mind.

With that caveat, let's turn to the central point of this chapter. There is something going on in this human experience that is best described as "the heart." The path of awakening is, as my teacher and friend Jack Kornfield has famously taught and written about, "a path with heart." The heart, like the mind and body, is not naturally in harmony with the realities of life. Furthermore, the untrained heart is controlled by the base instinctual drives of greed, hatred, and delusion. Therefore, Buddhism is not a "follow your heart" type of philosophy. Rather, it is a path of *training* your heart to respond with compassion, kindness, mercy, and forgiveness.

This path of training the heart is the ultimate goal of Buddhism. The Buddha referred to the untrained heart/mind as being like a wild monkey. The monkey heart tends to swing from emotion to emotion, from future to past, from one craving to the next. The practices touched on in this chapter (and developed more fully later) offer us ways to train the monkey, as it were. By training the monkey to chill out, to pay attention, to spend more time with wise thoughts and feelings and less with unwise, we give the monkey a refuge, a safe home, within ourselves. The monkey becomes less fearful, and with the feeling of safety comes the ability to see more clearly so that we can navigate our lives appropriately. The trained heart allows us to access the wise responses within—responses that bring about more happiness and less suffering.

I have come to believe that the states of generosity, compassion, loving-kindness, appreciation, forgiveness, and equanimity (balance) are natural by-products of the meditative path. I've also come to see the real importance of cultivating these qualities, of putting energy into a systematic and intentional cultivation of these heart/mind-states. Why wait until they arise spontaneously if some intentional uncovering can allow access to freedom more quickly?

The Buddha said in one teaching, "Abandon what is unskillful. One can abandon what is unskillful. If it were not possible, I would not ask you to do it. If abandoning that which is unskillful would cause harm, I would not ask you to do so, but as it brings benefit and happiness, therefore I say abandon it." He went on to say, "Cultivate the good. One can cultivate the good. If it were not possible, I would not ask you to do so. If this cultivation brought about harm, I would not ask you to do it. But as this cultivation of good brings benefit and happiness, I say cultivate it." By pursuing the heart/mind's deepest generosity, compassion, loving-kindness, appreciation, and equanimity through meditative practices and an appreciation of our interconnectedness with others, we learn to *abandon* or let go of unskillful mental states and *cultivate* skillful mental states.

For example, at first we may experience only how angry we are, but gradually we may begin to realize that the anger is fueled by fear. As in the example from the previous chapter, if we're driving down the road and another driver does something that endangers us—we get cut off, perhaps—we feel angry and maybe even yell at the other driver, punctuating a curse by giving the finger. But what has really happened is fear: we were afraid of being hurt, or afraid of our car being damaged. Fear is the *primary* emotion; anger is a *secondary* reaction to that fear. Our loving-kindness practice will teach us to be friendly to our fears, to treat the monkey with tenderness and mercy, and our compassion practice will allow us to respond with care to the suffering of fear and anger. Thus the unskillful mental states of fear and anger will be met with kindness and compassion.

This process of abandoning that which is unskillful or unwholesome happens gradually, over time. We don't just begin to practice and immediately let go of all unskillful attitudes. The process takes gradual, systematic training, though never by force. Training the monkey must be done over a long and gradual process of gently and lovingly encouraging the monkey to return to the heart. You don't have to wait to start training your heart; start now, by beginning to pay attention to your breath, body, mind, and emotions. Do your best to allow what arises in awareness to be met with kindness. More specific instructions will be offered later in the book, but it is never too early to begin turning your attention inward with kind intentions. Just as force is not the instigator, neither is fear. No, letting go happens when we begin to see, through present-time awareness, how painful the unskillful, unwholesome mind-states of anger, fear, greed, judgment, jealousy, selfishness, and lust really are—when we see that the actions that come from these mind-states are causing pain and/or suffering to ourselves and others.

The cultivation of wholesome mind-states is likewise gradual. When we begin to care about others and ourselves in a deeper way, then the friendliness and love and generosity that are innate within each of us begin to surface. As we stop cultivating the unwholesome and unskillful mind-states, as they gradually fade away, we begin cultivating the wholesome. Slowly, over years of practice, a transformation happens. Cultivating the good doesn't mean taking on virtue from outside ourselves; it means uncovering our own innate potential for love and connection—a potential that has been deeply buried and obscured through a lifetime of misinformation and not being taught the truth, through our own confused attempts to find happiness via sense pleasures, through hatred, through revenge, or through whatever our own particular top-ten confusions have been. Cultivating the good means uncovering or recovering the wisdom and compassion that are present as potential in *all* of us.

This means that we begin to align our intentions, actions, and mind-states with a vision of the awakened heart—with what the Mahayana Buddhists refer to as our "Buddha nature"— that is, the innate potential for awakening. There is a natural awakened aspect of the heart that is within all of us, though obscured. The good news is that it can be *un*obscured. How?

By walking the path. By putting into practice the values and theories that the Buddha taught and exemplified. By making the effort to abandon the unskillful and cultivate the good—and not just on the meditation mat but in all aspects of our lives. We begin with the intentional aspect of meditation, the formal sitting practice, but then we expand our intentionality to all aspects of our life, including the workplace and (perhaps the hardest and most important practice) our relationships.

The teachings in this book provide an in-depth map of your heart and a guide to bringing your heart into harmony with reality. The outcome of training your monkey will be a heart that radiates kindness, compassion, generosity, forgiveness, and love.

Chapter 3

INSPIRED TO REVOLT

faith: not what we believe but what
gets us motivated to act

Buddhism often claims not to ask for faith, but only to empower individuals to find out for themselves what is true. Although I feel that this is generally the case with Buddhism—indeed, I have often been guilty of preaching the nonfaith message of the Buddha—it seems important to admit that what's being taught and the practices that you're being encouraged to undertake do ask for some level of faith. Unlike many religious or spiritual paths, Buddhism is not asking you to believe in anything that you can never know for yourself, however. All of the Buddha's wisdom is available to you, verifiable in your own direct experience.

Through actions taken, we can experience for ourselves the verified truth of reality. However, it may take quite a while for us to clear away the confusion, conditioning, and ignorance that are blocking the liberating truth and happiness that Buddhism promises. In the meantime, we are asked to have some faith that the time and effort applied to our dharma practice—our attempts to train the monkey and thus to experience for ourselves the wisdom of the Buddha—will be worthwhile in the long run.

Despite Buddhism's nonfaith approach, the Buddha himself said at one point that faith was always the prerequisite for action on the spiritual path. We might substitute the word "confidence" or "inspiration" for "faith" in this case. The Buddha's comment came as he was explaining that, before his enlightenment, he met someone who inspired him: he encountered a guy who was committed to spiritual practice, and he noticed that the man seemed to be happier and have more meaning to his life than he himself did. The young Siddhartha (the Buddha's birth name) was inspired by that example to try meditation and spiritual principles; he had some *faith* that they were worth trying, and he had confidence in his own ability to train his mind and heart, to see through the religious dogma and experience liberating truth for himself. The faith that someone else inspired in him was the prerequisite for his inner revolution.

What brought *you* to the teachings and practices of Buddhism? What inspired *you* to begin reading about and practicing the revolutionary teachings of dharma? Was it a person you met, a book you read, a good acid trip, a bad acid trip, or something else? How much faith do you have in the Buddha's teachings? Does your response include some healthy skepticism and questioning, or have you accepted all of the dharma "on faith"? Or, if you are a veteran of the spiritual search, perhaps you have already verified the truth of the dharma through your own direct experience.

Faith, in this sense, is an important aspect of the path. My own experience with faith is that while I was incarcerated, in my late teens, I was skeptical about mindfulness meditation. Although I'd grown up around Buddhism, I didn't understand that particular practice. What was the good in sitting still? I had no faith that it could change anything. But after years of drug addiction, crime, and now incarceration, what did I have to lose? My mind was beginning to open to the possibility of a different path. It was through a conversation with my father, when he explained how mindfulness meditation could help me, that I was inspired to try it for myself. I was still very skeptical about Buddhism in the beginning, but I had some faith in my father. He inspired in me an inkling of willingness to give meditation a try. Much to my surprise and relief, I realized almost immediately after trying it that meditation was a useful tool. I suspected that I had only scratched the surface of what was possible with the application of mindfulness, but even that initial experience inspired confidence in the technique of meditation and, more generally, the path of the Buddha.

Our initial inspiration or faith in someone else—that necessary prerequisite—must always be replaced by a verified faith or confidence based on our own experience, however. It's that second component that most organized religion lacks, and that many dabblers in Buddhism ignore.

Something else about faith that seems important (and is often misunderstood) is the place of doubt and fear within the mind of a practitioner. Even the Buddha was susceptible to negative feelings. As mentioned earlier, even during the process of enlightenment, the Buddha continued to experience an aspect of his mind that he referred to as "Mara"—that aspect of the mind that experiences craving, aversion, and doubt. In fact, the Buddha's experience of enlightenment is the story of his battle with Mara. Mara attacks the Buddha with lust, with fear and violence, but when these fail to derail the Buddha from his resolve to awaken, Mara attacks with his most powerful weapon of all: doubt. The Buddha responds to each attack with wisdom and compassion. In response to doubt, the Buddha reflects on all the hard work he has done in the past; he inclines his mind and heart toward faith and confidence based on the progress that he has made so far.

The verified faith of the Buddha eventually won the battle with Mara, but their relationship was not over at that point. No, Mara continued to visit the Buddha throughout his life. Put another way, we could say that the Buddha continued to live with Mara as an aspect of his mind. Although he was free from the dictates of and misidentification with Mara as personal or powerful, the Buddha still had a human mind, and Mara continued to visit the Buddha. Mara came back regularly to see if the wisdom and compassion of the Buddha had wavered. Fear, desire, and doubt still arose in the enlightened Buddha's mind. The difference was that he responded every time with, "I see you, Mara." He did not take Mara's visitations personally and did not feel that he had to act on them; he saw fear, desire, and doubt as they were and responded with care and understanding.

The point here is that if the Buddha had to deal with doubt, then of course we are also going to have to deal with it. Doubt is not the absence of faith; it is just another aspect of the mind. Ultimately we have to learn how to allow faith and doubt to cohabitate. Becoming friendly with ourselves has to include every aspect of our being, including every manifestation of Mara. This gives us a much more practical and attainable definition of faith. What we're looking for isn't unquestioning acceptance of ideology or dogma, but the faith and confidence to persevere in the presence of doubt and fear.

The path of liberating the heart, of dharma practice, has been likened to a long and arduous trek through an unknown wilderness. At the beginning of our journey we meet someone or read about someone who has been on this same journey before us, who has gone through the wilderness of his or her own heart/mind and returned transformed, awakened, and at ease with all life. We are inspired; we have gained some faith that this journey is worth taking. We pack up our bags and head out along the path. In the beginning we are filled with the energy and exuberance of our faith, which drives us forward. For some this faith is sustained for a very long time; for others, after a short time the journey becomes increasingly difficult, and feelings of doubt begin to override feelings of faith. What seems to be true for everyone is that, at certain points along the way, we will face the attacks of Mara: we will feel lost in the desert or terrified in the haunted forests of our mind. These are the times when we need to reflect on our earlier faith, on the verified progress we have made. In these difficult times it is also important to remember that we were warned about these deserts and forests, to remember that the places that scare us, that seem hopelessly dangerous, are indications that we are getting closer to the destination. Often the fear is just Mara's (or the mind's) way of trying to keep us stuck in the safe but miserable norm of a survival-based existence.

Along the journey of awakening there will certainly be ebbs and flows in the amount of faith that we have. The key is to continue our forward momentum even on the days that we are experiencing more doubt than confidence.

Faith is good; doubt is natural. Proceed! The revolution awaits.

Part 2

THE MIDDLE PATH OF THE 1%ERS OF THE HEART

between the dead end of worldliness
and the dead end of religion

Chapter 4

MERCY: IT'S NOT JUST FOR THE GODS ANYMORE

the radical practice of nonharming

The term *mercy* is not often used in most schools of Buddhism, but I've found it to be an incredibly useful concept. Let's begin by defining it. My definition of mercy uses a verb form: "to stop hurting, to cease causing harm, to end suffering." The dictionary's definition is more along the lines of "compassion toward someone that you have power over." This latter definition is often used in a Western religious context in the sense of God having mercy on humans. But from a Buddhist perspective we are not interested in the concept of external powers or "God." We understand that we *all* have some level of power over ourselves—for example, that we have the power to cause harm to ourselves and others. So from a Buddhist perspective, showing mercy means having compassion for oneself and others; it means stopping harm or, at the very least, lessening the amount of suffering we cause.

The Buddha often said that his teachings had only the aim of ending suffering. I see this aim as synonymous with mercy. The Buddha's dharma is a path of mercy, a path of ending suffering through acts of compassion and wisdom. The Buddha is teaching us to be merciful with ourselves, each other, and this world.

In Buddhist circles there is much emphasis put on compassion, but as I have already stated, in the beginning I found compassion to be inaccessible. Although I found that I had very little capacity for a compassionate response in those early days, at times I did have the capacity to stop hurting myself. There were moments of mercy. Not much love, perhaps, but simply the willingness to stop causing harm. Showing mercy does not necessarily require responding to self or others with compassion; at times it is the step *before* compassion—a willingness to abstain from harmful actions, not out of love or compassion, but just out of self-preservation. Often we learn to tolerate pain before we can make the leap toward compassion.

And yet tolerating the unavoidable pains in life is itself an act of mercy, because *not* tolerating them causes suffering. Meditation teaches us this clearly. When we are sitting in meditative stillness and our bodies become uncomfortable, our tendency is to react by either trying to avoid or alleviate the pain, or pushing it away with anger and aversion. We wage war on pain. The anger we feel against our pain leads to another layer of suffering; in other words, the emotional suffering of hatred gets layered on top of the pain of sitting still. When we learn to meet our pain with tolerance, we end the emotional suffering of hatred. This is an act of mercy toward ourselves, a counter-instinctual rebellion.

As I learned to tolerate rather than hate my pains (physical, emotional, and mental), I saw that pain was nothing more than unpleasant sensory experience. It was resistance, fear, and hatred that caused real suffering. So then I began to have some mercy on myself. I began to pause in moments of difficulty, to be mindful of the sensations and tolerate them without reacting. At times when I tried to be compassionate I hit a steel wall in my heart; however, even if I was unable to access the tenderness of a loving heart, I was still experiencing some relief from suffering by not hating my pain so much—in other words, I was benefiting from mercy.

Mercy has a role beyond our relationship to pain, however. As stated above, showing mercy means ceasing to cause harm or having compassion. And as we all know, our suffering is not only about the pains and difficulties of life; we also create a tremendous amount of suffering through our relationship to pleasure. Our tendency is one of craving and clinging, as we saw in an earlier chapter. Our biological survival instinct constantly sends our mind and body cravings for pleasure to be obtained and sustained. We become attached to each pleasant thought, feeling, taste, smell, and sound. But because everything is impermanent, we're craving and clinging to *fleeting* experiences. Pleasure *never* lasts long enough; we can *never* sustain enough pleasure to satisfy the cravings. Suffering is the inevitable outcome of clinging to experiences that are unsustainable. Each moment of attachment or clinging creates some level of suffering in our lives as we grieve the loss of pleasure. What we often forget is that we have the power and ability simply to let go, and each moment of letting go is an act of mercy. The subversive act of nonclinging is an internal coup d'état.

When an alcoholic stops drinking, it is not because of a miracle or the grace of God. It's the result of an act of mercy on the self. When someone renounces *any* substance that is causing the self harm, he or she is being merciful.

Many years ago my friend and colleague Pablo Das was suffering from anxiety and panic attacks. Through his meditation and some wise counsel, he came to see that one of the main factors leading to his feelings of panic was his consumption of caffeine. He began to pay attention to how much coffee, soda, and chocolate he consumed. When he saw evidence that his anxiety was indeed fueled by caffeine, he stopped consuming caffeinated foods and beverages. His renunciation was an act of mercy: he was able to stop harming himself with those substances.

Mercy is a step in the right direction. Until we can uncover the love and compassion of our hearts, the practice of creating less harm, of being more merciful, may be the bulk of our practice.

Chapter 5

COMPASSION: THE WEAPON OF REAL REVOLUTIONARIES

the subversive act of uncovering
the antidote to suffering

As we train the heart, we move from understanding that pain is a given, to learning to tolerate pain and beginning to meet it with mercy. The next step is compassion. Our greatest salvation will come when we uncover compassion, when we learn to meet pain with love rather than hatred. The word that the Buddha used for compassion was *karuna*. It translates as "a movement in the heart, in response to pain." Compassion is very simply the experience of caring about pain and suffering—ours and others'.

As was noted earlier, pain is a given in life. We all experience pain, not just occasionally but daily. Pain is what we feel from the unpleasant experience itself—the sensation, emotion, thought, or experience that is received as unpleasant. For the untrained heart/mind, suffering is a given as well, in addition to pain. Suffering is the layer of resistance, anger, confusion, and despair that we create *in reaction to pain*. With practice, we can gain the ability to choose how to respond to pain, thus reducing our suffering.

Our instinctual tendency is to meet pain with aversion—in other words, to try to push pain away. Reflect for a moment: What is your first reaction to, say, stubbing your toe? Most of us tend to react either with aversion (trying to push the pain away) or denial (trying to pretend the pain isn't there). The experience of freedom comes when, through mindfulness, we begin to have a wise response to pain, a response that is not aversion but compassion. When we stub our toe, we can try to send love and compassion to the pain, instead of hatred; we can learn to soften to the pain rather than tensing up around it. As I said earlier, mercy is often a step toward compassion. Through practice we begin first to understand intellectually that pain is unavoidable. Then we begin to surrender the instinctual fight against the unavoidable pain we experience. Then we gain mercy toward pain by learning to accept and tolerate it. With that grounding, finally we have the possibility of meeting the accepted and tolerated pain with the heart's caring and loving response of compassion.

Compassion pertains to both our own pain and that of others, both the personal and the impersonal. For me, compassion has come from personal trial and error. For the first half of my life I tried to deny and run from pain. I wasn't very successful: no matter how many drugs I took, I always came down; no matter how much sex I had, it always ended; no matter how much attention I got, the loneliness returned. Pain always seemed to catch up with me. Eventually I had to accept that it's impossible to get rid of pain completely. Aversion, denial, anger, and suppression just don't work. Once I opened my mind to the possibility of compassion and explored the Buddha's practices, I saw for myself that when I related to pain with friendliness and care, rather than fear and avoidance, pain was much more manageable and seemed to pass more quickly. Trying to push away physical or emotional pain is like creating a dam for the impermanent experience: it doesn't get rid of the pain; it simply keeps it backed up. Eventually the floodgates burst, however, and we are faced with the truth of our self-made suffering.

Compassion isn't a soft and easy practice, though everyday connotations of the word might suggest that. Anger and aversion are easy. Compassion, on the other hand, is hard core, the antidote to suffering. It's a very practical and applicable relationship to life's difficulties. Compassion isn't our only option, of course, when we encounter pain—and for most it isn't our first instinct—but it's the only option that works to free us from suffering.

Many find that compassion comes more easily toward the suffering of others than toward that of the self. Although it is a noble and wise experience to care for the suffering and pain of others, our caring will not end our suffering, or theirs. The end of suffering will come only when we meet our *own* pain with compassion. When we are committed to the path of nonharming, when we are living in harmony with the principles we wish to see in the world, then our compassion will be genuine, grounded in the true potential for freedom rather than in a deluded wish for pain to go away.

Remember, though, that compassion does not mean getting rid of pain—or at least not always. Because some of the pain we experience is necessary and important, we don't want to get stuck in the aversive tendency of trying to end all the pain in the world. Pain is usually not the problem; it is hatred of pain that is the real problem, causing the overlay of suffering that I mentioned earlier. Some people use the word *compassion* as a thinly veiled excuse for aversion. For example, in meditation people sometimes will say that out of compassion for themselves they had to shift posture during a sitting practice period. That isn't compassion at work; that's aversion to pain. Now, there is nothing wrong with being gentle and patient with our ability to tolerate pain. I'm certainly not encouraging a macho, "sit still no matter what" attitude. But it is important to be clear: acting out of aversion is not the same as acting out of compassion, and eventually we do need to gain the ability to sit still and allow ourselves to have some insight into the impermanent nature of pain.

In California these days we have a lot of talk about medical marijuana, and the dispensaries of that medication are often called "compassion clubs." But it is my understanding that only a tiny percentage of the "compassion club" members have any medical issue. The vast majority are suffering only from the affliction of craving a good high and from an aversion to reality. Getting high is not a compassionate act; it is a temporary avoidance technique. Now, for those who are using the weed as medicine and finding that it helps alleviate some of the painful symptoms of their illness, *that* is a form of mercy—a compassionate act—that I fully support. My point here is that escaping reality is not an expression of true compassion; true compassion means facing reality and transforming our relationship to it. This need to face reality is probably part of the reason that the Buddha always encouraged a drug-and-alcohol-free lifestyle for his students. Drinking and drugs are just other forms and tools of aversion and craving. The Buddha asks us to consider, out of compassion for ourselves, giving up false pleasures such as drinking and getting high—pleasures that serve nothing positive and can only slow down our journey toward a liberated heart.

I truly believe that compassion will come to us with time and intentional effort in the direction of caring about our pain. Our heart needs to be guided in this direction, however. One of the best ways to train our heart/mind is through the discipline of meditation. Below I've provided instructions on how to meditate on compassion.

Compassion Meditation Instructions

- Find a comfortable place to sit, and allow your attention to settle into the present-time experience of the body. Relax any physical tension that is being held in the body by softening the belly; relax the eyes and jaw and allow your shoulders to naturally fall away from the head.

- After a short period of settling into present-time awareness, begin to reflect on your deepest desire for happiness and freedom from suffering. Allow your heart's truest longing for truth and well-being to come into consciousness.

- With each breath, breathe into the heart's center the acknowledgment of your wish to be free from harm, to be safe and protected, and to experience compassion for all beings.

- Slowly begin to *offer yourself compassionate phrases,* with the intention to uncover the heart's sometimes-hidden caring and friendly response. Your phrases can be as simple as the following:

  > "May I learn to care about suffering and confusion."

  > "May I respond with mercy and empathy to pain."

  > "May I be filled with compassion."

  If those phrases do not mean anything to you, create your own words to meditate on. Find a few simple phrases that have a compassionate and merciful intention and slowly begin to offer these well-wishings to yourself.

- As you sit in meditation repeating these phrases in your mind, your attention will be drawn back, as in mindfulness meditation, into thinking about other things or resisting and judging the practice or your capacity for compassion. It takes a gentle and persistent effort to return to the next phrase each time the attention wanders:

"May I learn to care about suffering and confusion."

Feel the breath and the body's response to each phrase.

"May I respond to pain with mercy and empathy."

Notice where the mind goes with each phrase.

"May I be filled with compassion."

Allow the mind and body to relax into the reverberations of each phrase.

Simply repeat these phrases over and over to yourself as a kind of mantra or statement of positive intention. But don't expect to instantly feel compassionate through this practice. Sometimes all we see is our lack of compassion and the judging mind's resistance. Simply acknowledge what is happening and continue to repeat the phrases, being as friendly and merciful with yourself as possible in the process.

- After a few minutes of sending these compassionate phrases to yourself, bring your attention back to your breath and body, again relaxing into the posture. Then bring to mind *someone who has been beneficial for you to know or know of,* someone who has inspired you or shown you great compassion. Recognizing that just as you wish to be cared for and understood, that benefactor likewise shares the universal desire to be met with compassion, begin offering him or her the caring phrases. Slowly repeat each phrase with that person in mind as the object of your well-wishing:

> "Just as I wish to learn to care about suffering and confusion, to respond to pain with mercy and empathy, and to be filled with compassion, may you learn to care about suffering and confusion."
>
> "May you respond to pain with mercy and empathy."
>
> "May you be filled with compassion."

Continue offering these phrases from your heart to your benefactor's, developing the feeling of compassion in relationship to the pain of others.

- When the mind gets lost in a story, memory, or fantasy, simply return to the practice. Begin again offering mercy and care to the benefactor.

- After a few minutes of sending compassion to the benefactor, let him or her go and return to your direct experience of the breath and body. Pay extra attention to your heart or emotional experience. Then bring to mind someone whom you do not know well, *someone who is neutral* (someone you neither love nor hate—perhaps someone you don't know at all, a person you saw during your day, walking down the street or waiting in line at the market). With the understanding that the desire for freedom from suffering is universal, begin offering that neutral person the compassionate phrases:

"May you learn to care about suffering and confusion."

"May you respond to pain with mercy and empathy."

"May you be filled with compassion."

- After a few minutes of sending compassion to the neutral person, bring attention back to your breath and body. Then expand the practice to include *family and friends toward whom your feelings may be mixed*—both loving and judgmental:

"May you all learn to care about suffering and confusion."

"May you all respond to pain with mercy and empathy."

"May you all be filled with compassion."

- After a few minutes of sending compassion to the mixed category, bring attention back to your breath and body.

- Then expand the practice to include the *difficult people in your life and in the world.* (By *difficult* I mean those whom you have put out of your heart, those toward whom you hold resentment.) With even the most basic understanding of human nature, it will become clear that all beings wish to be met with compassion; all beings—even the annoying, unskillful, violent, confused, and unkind—wish to be free from suffering. With this in mind, and with the intention to free yourself from hatred, fear, and ill will, allow someone who is a source of difficulty in your mind or heart to be the object of your compassion meditation, meeting that person with the same phrases and paying close attention to your heart/mind's response:

> "May you learn to care about suffering and confusion."

> "May you respond to pain with mercy and empathy."

> "May you be filled with compassion."

- After a few minutes of practice in the direction of difficult people, begin to expand the field of compassion to *all those who are in your immediate vicinity.* Start by sending compassionate phrases to anyone in your home or building at the time of practice. Then gradually expand to *those in your town or city,* allowing your positive intention for meeting everyone with compassion to spread out in all directions. Imagine covering *the whole world* with these positive thoughts. Send compassion to the north and south, east and west. Radiate an open heart and fearless mind to all beings in existence—those above and below, the seen and the unseen, those being born and those who are dying. With a boundless and friendly intention, begin to repeat the phrases:

"May all beings learn to care about suffering and confusion."

"May all beings respond to pain with mercy and empathy."

"May all beings be filled with compassion."

- After a few minutes of sending compassion to all beings everywhere, simply let go of the phrases and bring attention back to your breath and body, investigating the sensations and emotions that are present now. Then, whenever you are ready, allow your eyes to open and your attention to come back to your surroundings.

Chapter 6

HURT PEOPLE HURT PEOPLE

forgiveness: no more drinking poison
and expecting your enemies to die

I remember the day that I realized I had finally forgiven everyone for everything. I had been doing the forgiveness practices of repeating phrases of forgiveness toward myself, toward those who had harmed me, and toward those whom I had harmed for over ten years at that point. It had been a long and often painful process of letting go.

My heart had been heavily defended for most of my life. When I was a child my life had become so painful and confusing that I was suicidal. My parents divorced when I was two years old and my sister was four. My mother, who had primary custody after the divorce, was struggling with addiction, and my father, though still in the picture, was often unavailable

due to his own commitments to meditation and teaching. My
mother remarried and had twins when I was five. My stepfather was abusive to her, to me and my sister, and eventually to
his own children. It was around that time that I began to contemplate killing myself.

With the birth of my younger brother and sister—the
twins—it felt clear to me that there wasn't enough attention
and love to go around. I felt left out, abandoned, and all alone.
Suicide was my security blanket, my get-out-of-jail-free card.
Saving that card until it was needed, I developed day-to-day
survival skills: I learned to close my heart. I learned to shut
down my emotional needs, to push away the feelings of vul-
nerability. That need for emotional distance was what led me,
within just a few more years, to start smoking, drinking, and
getting high. I discovered early on that drugs took the edge off
my feelings of despair and loneliness. Suppressing my pain the
only ways I knew how, I began acting out—lighting fires, steal-
ing, lying, and even becoming violent.

I began to hate. I hated adults. I hated teachers. I hated
cops. I hated hippies. I hated my siblings. I hated Carter. I
hated Reagan. I hated Bush—both of them. I hated people with
money. I hated happy people. I hated depressed people. I hated
the world. Eventually I found an outlet for my hatred in the
punk scene. Reveling in all that hatred, I acted out even more:
I fought. I stole. I lied. I got high. I got drunk. I got in lots of
trouble. I smoked PCP. I ate lots of acid. I got strung out on
crack. I shot heroin. Through all this, I hated myself and who I
had become. I was seventeen years old.

While in jail for my third felony arrest at that young age, at my father's suggestion I began to meditate. That practice gave me the determination and strength to stop taking drugs and drinking. I turned my attention inward and began the process of healing—a process that continues to this day.

Ten years into my meditation practice, that moment of freedom from all conscious resentment and ill will toward anyone, living or dead, was the first time in my life that I truly understood the Buddha's teachings on loving-kindness. But along with that insight into the potential of an unconditionally loving heart came a delusion: I thought that I would feel that way forever. Despite my studies of the Buddha's dharma, I somehow retained the mistaken view of permanence. I had been working hard for freedom; once I experienced a moment of it, I expected it to last. But like everything else in this heart/mind and world, that flash of forgiveness was impermanent.

The experience of forgiveness is a momentary release. In reality, we don't (and can't) forgive forever, only for that present moment. This is both good and bad news. The good part is that we can stop judging ourselves for our inability to let go of resentments once and for all, completely and absolutely. We forgive in one moment and become resentful again in the next. It is not a failure to forgive; it is just a failure to understand impermanence. The bad news is that forgiveness is not something that we will ever be done with; it is an ongoing aspect of our lives, and thus it necessitates a vigilant practice of moment-to-moment letting go.

Although it has been over ten years since that first moment of freedom from the pains and resentments of my past, I still practice forgiveness on a daily basis. Now it is no longer a chore: it has become a simple and natural way of responding to my heart/mind when feelings of hurt, fear, injustice, or betrayal arise. I now understand that freedom from these negative feelings is not a distant goal, but is available right here in this moment. If I let go and respond with compassion and forgiveness, I will be free. If I continue to grasp at and wallow in my painful righteousness, I will continue to suffer. And of course at times I *do* still choose the path of suffering—but less and less. Knowing that freedom is readily available has drastically changed my life. I no longer have to tolerate unnecessary sorrow.

I share this with you to let you know that if I can do this practice, so can you. But before I go too much further, let me back up and break down some of the basics of the forgiveness practice.

Forgiveness—the journey and practice of intentionally letting go of the stuff of the past that has caused us emotional suffering and feelings of anger and resentment—begins with the understanding that all harm caused comes out of suffering and ignorance. There is no such thing as wise abuse or enlightened betrayal. This is the core truth of harm: it always comes from confusion and suffering. Anger, violence, and all forms of abuse and betrayal are always motivated by an ignorant or confused intention. When the mind is *un*confused—awakened—it cannot intentionally cause malicious harm. The awakened heart/mind acts with only wisdom and compassion. That understanding is essential as we practice forgiveness, in that it forces us to distinguish between the confused, suffering actors and the actions themselves.

This is perhaps the most essential perspective in forgiveness: the separation of actor from action. Whether the harm that requires forgiveness was an unskillful act we carried out that hurt someone else, or an unskillful act on the part of another that we felt victimized by, we must see that the action and the actor are not the same thing. Most of the time the anger and resentment we hold are directed against the actor; in our minds we don't instinctively separate the abuser from the abuse. But this is exactly what we *must* do. We must come to the understanding that confusion comes and goes. An action from a confused and suffering being in the past doesn't represent who that being is forever; it is only an expression of that being's suffering. Furthermore, if we cling to resentment over past hurts, we simply increase our own suffering. By holding on to our anger and resentments, we make our own lives more difficult than need be.

This in no way means that we should subject ourselves or others to repeated or further abuse. Part of the forgiveness and healing process is to create healthy boundaries. We might, for example, forgive someone but choose never to interact with that person again. We must not confuse letting go of past injuries with feeling an obligation to let the injurers back into our life. The freedom of forgiveness often includes a firm boundary and loving distance from those who have harmed us. We may likewise need to keep a loving distance from those whom we have harmed, to keep them from further harm. To that extent, this practice of letting go of the past and making amends for our behavior is more internal work than relational. As my father likes to say, "We can let them back into our heart without ever letting them back into our house."

Forgiveness is not just a selfish pursuit of personal satisfaction or righteousness. It actually alleviates the amount of suffering in the world. As each one of us frees ourselves from clinging to resentments that cause suffering, we relieve our friends, family, and community of the burden of our unhappiness. This is not a philosophical proposal; it is a verifiable and practical truth. Through our suffering and lack of forgiveness, we tend to do all kinds of unskillful things that hurt others. We close ourselves off from love, for example, out of fear of further pains or betrayals. This alone—a lack of openness to the love shown to us—is a way that we cause harm to our loved ones. The closed heart lets no one in or out.

Early on in my own meditation practice, I clearly saw that I had been in a lot of pain for a long time and that my pain had affected others in incredibly unskillful ways. Then I began to see that the people toward whom I had been holding resentment had also been in pain and that they had spilled their pain onto me.

This allowed me to begin to separate the person from the action and truly see the confused human being behind the hurt. This was the hardest part: not associating the people with their actions, but seeing them as confused human beings trying their best and failing miserably, just as I had. I found trying to adopt that attitude toward *everyone* in my life incredibly challenging. It took years of trying and failing to come to a real sense of this understanding.

This long-term effort is a common experience, because for-giveness can't be forced. By holding on to anger and resentment for years or even decades, we allow that reaction to become habitual. And habits take time and intentional action to break. In forgiveness we are actually retraining our heart/mind to respond in a new and more beneficial way. By separating the actor from the action, we are getting to the root of the suffer-ing, both caused and experienced. Unfortunately, forgiveness is a counterintuitive process. Our biological instinct is to respond to all forms of pain with aversion, anger, hatred, and resent-ment. As noted earlier, this is the basic survival instinct of the human animal. It works quite well to protect us from *external* harm, yet it seems to create *inner* harm. Forgiveness is the quite deliberate process of freeing ourselves from internal suffering, and helping to free others of theirs.

A common feeling among many of us who have felt injured by others is that forgiveness is a gift that the offender has not earned. Yet does our lack of forgiveness really punish them, or does it just make our own hearts hard and our own lives unpleasant? Is forgiveness a gift to others or to oneself? Perhaps both. Let's take a closer look at forgiveness, moving from forgiv-ing ourselves to forgiving others.

Seeking Forgiveness from Self and Others

Contrary to what one might expect, forgiving ourselves is often the hardest type of forgiveness. We are stuck with a mind that is quick to judge, bent toward comparison, jealousy, and fear.

To forgive ourselves we must change our relationship to our own mind—a radical concept. We cannot *stop* the judging mind; thus our best bet is to change our relationship to it. Mindfulness shows us that most of what is happening in our mind is nonvolitional, not intentional; it happens all by itself. That's a hugely important point—indeed, the first step toward forgiving ourselves is understanding that the mind is not under our full control. Understanding this, we can then begin to influence our relationship to the mind. This gradual change in how we relate to the thinking mind leads to a change in how we relate to the past, to the anger we've been holding on to, and to ourselves.

We are stuck with ourselves for a lifetime, so we might as well find the best way of understanding and accepting the pains of the past. It is in our best interest, and the most beneficial thing we can do for others as well, to find a way to meet ourselves with compassion rather than resentment. Though this sounds simple and straightforward, forgiving oneself is often the most difficult work of a lifetime. It is also the most important.

It helps if we investigate our mind's tendency to judge and criticize ourselves, paying special attention to any feelings of unworthiness or self-hatred. If we can bring a friendly awareness to our mind's fears and resentments, we may discover that our mind is actually just trying to protect us from further harm. The barrage of fears and insecurities may be a psychological defense mechanism, an attempt to avoid future harm—though a confused attempt, of course, because resentment and anger toward oneself never lead to happiness. But if we can understand and accept that we have been confused, we may find it easier to begin to meet ourselves with mercy and forgiveness, responding to the judging mind with the sort of gentle patience and understanding that we would show a sick and confused friend.

As I began the long process of forgiveness, I found it much easier to forgive myself as a confused child than to approach my adult pain. Recognizing that, I placed a picture of myself as a child on the altar where I meditate. Every day when I practiced meditation, I sent forgiveness to that kid who became the man who had experienced and caused great harm. Gradually, I became friendly with the child in the photograph. I began to care about him and all the confusion he experienced. Eventually, I was able to forgive him—the younger version of me—for allowing his confusion to hurt me and so many others. From that place of understanding and mercy, I was then able to grant my adult self that same forgiveness.

Forgiving ourselves is not the end of the process, though; it is just the beginning—or more likely just another piece of the puzzle. It is equally important that we let go of the shame we have been holding on to for having hurt others. If we go back through our lives and bring to mind everyone to whom we have caused harm, taking full responsibility and asking for forgiveness, that process of forgiveness will allow us to let go of our guilt and shame, which in turn will help us forgive others. When we humbly accept that at times in our life we have been the aggressor or abandoner or unkind one, and we see that every time it was because of our own suffering and confusion, we learn to see that those who hurt us were similarly confused.

Our self-understanding makes accessing compassion for our enemies a little easier.

But why, you may ask, should we rid ourselves of guilt and shame when we know that we have wronged someone? Aren't guilt and shame the very things we *should* be feeling? Well, no, because guilt and shame are judgments, carrying feelings of negativity and condemnation. Regret, on the other hand, is a discernment: there is no negative judgment, just a clear and honest appraisal of the past. When we have caused harm by being unskillful, regret is a healthy and desirable response. We *should* regret having caused harm. But feeling *ashamed* of the past is going a step too far; it's making the assessment that we are bad people. We are *not* bad people; we have simply acted inadvisably in relationship to our pains, cravings, and confusion. We have been hurting and have allowed our hurts to hurt others. A line from a movie I saw recently has stuck with me: "Hurt people hurt people." This becomes more and more clear as we deepen our practice of forgiveness.

Asking for forgiveness is an act of humility, generosity, and healing. Some level of regret will remain—and should—but shame and guilt will eventually disappear. Through structured meditation, we can train the heart/mind to let go, to meet past pains with understanding and acceptance.

Most of us must take self-forgiveness a step further. After doing the inner work of letting go, we must also take direct relational action. The process of releasing the heart/mind's grasp on past pains and betrayals almost always includes not just offering forgiveness to oneself, but also communicating with those whom we have harmed and making amends (that is, trying to make things right, whether simply through an apology or through some additional action). This takes great courage and a willingness to humbly accept full responsibility for our past actions. My experience is that this courage comes when we become dissatisfied enough with a life ruled by resentment and/or shame. The more we meditate, the more sensitive we become to the subtle agitation of resentments and guilt. From the wise desire for happiness and freedom stems the energy to humble ourselves, ask for forgiveness, and make amends.

I can't say it often enough: forgiveness is a process that continues throughout our life. We can't just say the phrases or do the meditation a couple times and be done with it. We can't just decide to forgive and magically let go of all our past pains and resentments. I've been working on this for over twenty years now, and I'm far from finished. In the early days, it was all the big stuff—people I had stolen from, hurt, betrayed, especially my parents and siblings. It was almost a full-time job asking everyone for forgiveness for all of the ways that I had caused them harm. There were some major healings in many of those conversations. As I made amends to my father, for example, he also asked me for forgiveness, admitting that he had not always been able to be there for me in the ways I needed. As I made amends to my stepmom, I was also able to express to her how much I loved her and how I felt in many ways that her loving presence in my life had saved me from an early death. Knocking on the doors of homes that I had robbed and approaching people that I had fought with took great courage, a courage that was fueled by my search for freedom. Almost all of the direct amends that I made were healing; they set me free from the past. They also tended to be healing for the people that I made amends to. People were grateful to hear that it wasn't their fault, that on many levels it was often not personal. A few times my amends were not accepted or appreciated. Some of the people that I had harmed were not open to my amends, they were not interested in speaking to me, or if they allowed a conversation they were still so hurt by what I had done that they just told me to fuck off. When that happened it hurt, but I understood and took the response as karma for my actions. I did not retaliate or push the issue, because it was time for me to let go internally and to continue my inner work of forgiving myself and others.

These days I still occasionally have to make amends, because I still catch myself acting out of fear, anger, or pride in ways that cause harm. When I do so, I try to ask for forgiveness as soon as possible. Consider this example. Recently I was teaching a meditation retreat with a teacher that I have very different views from. She and I began, in that retreat, to have some conflict about what is and isn't "real dharma." I got stuck in my own ideas and views and began to be critical and unkind to her. There is a wise way to disagree about such things, but I wasn't coming from that place. I was being judgmental and at times even mean; I was being unskillful and justifying it by gussying it up as self-righteousness. When it became clear that I was causing harm, I woke up. I stopped the bickering and judgmentalism and I made amends. I still thought I was right and she was wrong, but that was no longer the point. I had acted unwisely, and I asked for forgiveness for the way I had treated her.

Even as I asked her to forgive me for acting unskillfully, I forgave her for what I perceived as holding on to delusional views. Sometimes it's as simple as the saying has it: "Do you wanna be right, or do you wanna be happy?" Personally, I wanna be both! However, I do think we can find a balance, just as the Buddha did. In the oldest recorded teachings of the Buddha, he is often portrayed having conflict with people who came to question his teachings. He is able to say clearly that he thinks that the views held by some of his questioners are delusional, but he never says it in a mean or malicious way. He never has to go back and make amends. That is my goal with all of this: to live a life that is clean and ethical and to speak in a way that is honest but also kind; and when I fail, as I did at that recent retreat, to ask for forgiveness and make amends as soon as possible.

Forgiving Others

Forgiving the people that we have been holding resentment toward is the final step in the process. Hopefully we have gained some insight into why people hurt each other by now. Our enemies are not evil or bad people; they are just confused and hurting. If they weren't so confused, they wouldn't have done the unskillful things that we've been angry about. So our forgiveness is focused on having compassion for the suffering of greed, hatred, and delusion that motivated the harms caused. This is where it becomes most important to be able to separate the actor(s)—the person or perhaps group of people or even institution that we are resentful toward—from the action. If we look closely and get a little creative in our imagination, it is usually not hard to see that the actors were suffering from some form of greed, hatred, or delusion when they did what they did that hurt us. We affirm this understanding by looking closely at our own lives, at all of the times when we have hurt others simply because we did not know how to tolerate the pain or confusion in our lives, were motivated by greed or hatred, or were so "asleep" that we were delusional. In this light it becomes easier to see our enemies not as bad or evil, but as suffering and confused beings, and to feel compassion for the suffering that motivated the harms perpetrated—in other words, to forgive the actors.

Some actions may not be forgivable, but *all actors are.* For each actor, the person whose own suffering has spilled onto other people, there is always the possibility of compassion. There is always potential for mercy toward the suffering and confused person that hurts another.

While some resentments seem to vanish forever when we experience a moment of forgiveness, others return again and again. The most important thing to remember is that we must live in the present; and if in the present moment we are still holding on to old wounds and betrayals, it is in *this moment* that forgiveness is called for. With each temporary experience of forgiveness, deeper levels of hurt may be revealed. If and when that happens, we have the tools to forgive again and again.

Sitting here now, over twenty years into my meditation practice, I can honestly say that I am often free from resentment and ill will. I am often able to live from a perspective of compassion, mercy, and forgiveness. I am certainly neither perfect nor enlightened, but I can assure you that the path of forgiveness is one worth undertaking. It is from this place of personal experience that I encourage you to join me on this journey, to be part of the 1%ers of the heart.

Forgiveness Meditation Instructions

For this formal forgiveness practice it may be helpful to create an altar. It needn't be a physical structure: it could be just a corner of the room, for example. Alternatively, it could be a small table on which you place some photographs or objects that remind you of your intention to forgive.

- Find a comfortable place to sit, facing the altar (if you created one). Relax into the sitting posture. Take a few moments to settle into the position by intentionally releasing any held tension in your face, neck, shoulders, chest, or abdomen. Bring your attention to the present moment, focusing on each breath as it goes in and out.

- After settling into the present-time experience of sitting with awareness of the breath, allow the breath to come and go from your heart's center. Imagine breathing directly in and out of your heart.

- Feel what is present in your heart/mind and begin to set your intention to let go of the past by letting go of resentments. Say the word *forgiveness* in your mind and acknowledge how it feels to consider letting go.

- When you are ready, bring to mind some of the *ways that you have harmed others,* have betrayed or abandoned them. Include both the intentional and unintentional acts of harm you have participated in. Acknowledge and feel the anger, pain, fear, or confusion that motivated your actions.

- Begin to ask for forgiveness from those you have harmed:

    "I ask for your forgiveness."

    "Please forgive me for having caused you harm."

    "I now understand that I was unskillful and that my actions hurt you, and I ask for your forgiveness."

    Pause between each phrase, bringing attention to your heart/mind/body's reactions to these practices. Feel the feelings that arise, or the lack of feeling. Acknowledge the desire to be forgiven.

- If the mind gets too lost in the story and begins rationalizing and blaming, simply bring your attention back

to the breath and body in the present moment; then
continue repeating the phrases:

> "I ask for your forgiveness."

> "Please forgive me for having caused you harm."

> "I now understand that I was unskillful and
> that my actions hurt you, and I ask for your
> forgiveness."

- Spend some time repeating these phrases and reflect-
  ing on your past unskillfulness, remembering to soften
  your belly when it gets tight with judgment or fear.

- Relax back into breathing in and out of your heart's
  center. Take a few moments to let go of the last aspect
  of the exercise.

- Now begin to reflect on all of the *ways in which you have
  been harmed* in this lifetime. Remember that you are
  attempting to forgive the actors, not the actions, and
  that just as you have been confused and unskillful at
  times, those who hurt you were likewise suffering or
  confused.

- Bring to mind and invite back into your heart *those who
  have caused you harm*. With as much mercy and compassion as possible, begin offering forgiveness to those
  who have harmed you, those whom you have been
  holding resentment toward, with these same phrases:

> "I forgive you."

"I forgive you for all of the ways that you have caused me harm."

"I now offer you forgiveness, whether the hurt came through your actions, thoughts, or words."

"I know that you are responsible for your actions, and I offer you forgiveness."

- Pause between each phrase, bringing attention to your heart/mind/body's reactions to these practices. Feel the feelings that arise, or the lack of feeling. Acknowledge the desire to forgive.

- If the mind gets too lost in the story and begins ratio-nalizing and blaming, simply bring the attention back to the breath and body in the present moment; then begin repeating the phrases:

  "I forgive you."

  "I forgive you for all of the ways that you have caused me harm."

  "I now offer you forgiveness, whether the hurt came through your actions, thoughts, or words."

  "I know that you are responsible for your actions, and I offer you forgiveness."

- After some time of experiencing forgiveness, let go of the phrases and bring attention back to your direct experience of the present moment, feeling the breath as it comes and goes, softening the belly, and relaxing into the present. Attempt to let go of all levels of this exercise, relaxing back into the experience of your breath at the heart's center.

- When you are ready, let go of the reflection on those that have harmed you and bring your awareness back to yourself. Relax back into breathing in and out of your heart's center. Take a few moments to let go of the last aspect of the exercise.

- When you are ready, begin to reflect on yourself. Acknowledge all of the ways that you have harmed yourself. Contemplate your life and your thoughts, feelings, and actions toward yourself. Allow a heartfelt experience of the judgmental and critical feelings you carry toward yourself. Just as we have harmed others, there are so many ways that we have hurt ourselves. We have betrayed and abandoned ourselves many times, through our thoughts, words, and deeds—sometimes intentionally, often unintentionally.

- Begin to feel the physical and mental experience of sorrow and grief for yourself and the confusion in your life. Breathing into each moment, with each feeling that arises, soften and begin to invite yourself back into your heart. Allow forgiveness to arise.

- Picture yourself now, or at any time in your life, and reflect on all of the *ways in which you have judged, criticized, and caused emotional or physical harm to yourself.* With as much mercy and compassion as possible, begin to offer yourself forgiveness, perhaps picturing yourself as a child and inviting the disowned aspects of yourself back into your heart:

"I forgive you."

"I forgive you for all of the ways that you have caused me harm."

"I now offer you forgiveness, whether the hurt came through my actions, thoughts, or words."

"I know that I am responsible for my actions, and I offer myself forgiveness."

- Pause between each phrase, bringing attention to your heart/mind/body's reactions to these practices. Feel the feelings that arise, or the lack of feelings. Acknowledge the desire to be forgiven.

- If the mind gets too lost in the story and begins rationalizing and blaming, simply bring the attention back to the breath and body in the present moment; then begin repeating the phrases:

"I forgive you."

"I forgive you for all of the ways that you have caused me harm."

"I now offer you forgiveness, whether the hurt came through my actions, thoughts, or words."

"I know that I am responsible for my actions, and I offer myself forgiveness."

- Send yourself a moment of gratitude for trying to free yourself from the long-held resentments that make life more difficult than it needs to be.

- When you are ready, allow your eyes to open and attention to come back into the room or space you are in.

Chapter 7

HEART. CORE. LOVE.

the hard-core challenges of loving in this world of constant change

One core aspect of the heart is love. Love is experienced on several different levels. There is the *personal love* that we feel for our relatives and friends. There is the *romantic love* we experience in our sexually intimate relationships. Lastly, and most important to our heart's freedom, is *universal love* (or *unconditional loving-kindness*). In this chapter we'll look at the first two types of love, saving loving-kindness for the next chapter.

Personal Love

Personal love is a natural aspect of our developed evolution as living beings. In ideal circumstances we bond with and love our parents, siblings, and close friends. Not surprisingly, though, with *personal* love we tend to take everything very *personally*. As an example, when our mom or dad is not behaving the way we want them to, we may withdraw our love and replace it with anger, sadness, or some other negative reaction. Personal love tends to be very conditional: if our friends and relatives are being loving, we love them in return. If they are being mean or selfish, we are tempted to react in kind and may eventually stop loving them altogether—indeed, we may even begin to hate those same people that we once loved.

Personal love tends to lack wisdom, because it is ruled by the human survival instinct. (Yes, here it is again!) Our survival instinct, as you will recall by now, is born loving pleasure and all who provide it and hating pain and all who cause it. What most people call *love* is simply a built-in biological survival instinct. We seek what is pleasurable, nurturing, and sustaining, and we have little or no tolerance for pain. This is why in one moment I can love you (when I am getting what I want) and in the next moment I can hate you (when you are no longer paying enough attention to me). Personal love is fickle and conditional, it reflects very little personal effort, it lacks forgiveness, and it doesn't understand impermanence. If our experience with a parent, sibling, or friend is painful enough, we will close our heart to them completely.

Our families are always a mixture of pleasant and unpleasant experiences, of course, but the ruling force of personal love in the home always leans toward pleasure-providers. On this base level I am talking about the pleasures of food, shelter, attention, kindness, and shiny toys. Certainly many of us experienced the tragic event of getting our wires crossed as youngsters when a parent or other primary caregiver didn't provide us with the kind of attention or kindness that we needed. Those crossed wires in childhood create in adults a pattern of seeking love from people and situations that cannot provide it. This is one of the tragic flaws in the evolution of the human heart/mind: those of us who experienced an early betrayal of the parental bond have a tendency to accept (and even look for!) relationships that are more painful than pleasurable, rather than seeking out people who could and actually would pay attention to us, meet us with kindness, and love us.

I experienced firsthand the truth of getting stuck in patterns of unhealthy relationships. My early childhood conditioning from a mother who was struggling with addiction, working through two broken marriages, and trying her best to raise four children left me with confused ideas about love and relationships. As an adult I found myself repeatedly seeking love from emotionally unavailable women. My search for intimacy had become a quest to heal an old wound. Being unmet in relationships was a painfully familiar feeling—one so dominant that it was driving my choices in partners. From the outside it may have looked as if I liked pain. And perhaps part of me did; it was familiar, after all—so much like my childhood.

The good news is that dharma practice has the power to end the cycle of compulsively retraumatizing the heart's longing for love. As I practiced forgiving myself and others, I began to experience a change in my relationships. I stopped seeking the unavailable and started to feel that I actually deserved a love that was present, available, and open to real intimacy. Slowly progressing in my relationship choices, I eventually found a woman to spend my life with who was not just a substitute for Mommy. My wife and I have been together just four years now, but I know for certain that all of the happiness and joy we share is available to me only because of the dharma practice that has healed my heart.

The Buddhist practices of mindfulness, forgiveness, compassion, and loving-kindness do a tremendous amount of good for personal love relationships. Unless we train the mind and heart through meditative discipline, our love will stay limited and conditional forever. But with some effort, and with the wisdom that arises through meditation, the heart's capacity for love will grow and grow, eventually expanding to the ability to stay loving in the midst of painful situations. Of course, no matter how open, loving, and intimate we become, relationships are still at times going to be painful. That is the nature of personal love: in this world of constant change, of instinctual drives for pleasure, along with our individualized desires, at times we *do* experience the pain of attachment, aversion, and grief. In personal love relationships, we tend to cling—and clinging is by nature painful. If we work at it, though, compassion helps us stay loving even when we are not getting what we want. When we intentionally cultivate compassion, along with mercy, kindness, and forgiveness, our experience of personal love begins to meld into the realm of unconditional love.

Romantic Love

Because the craving for pleasure is at the center of our human experience, it is no accident that sexuality is one of the most pleasurable experiences available to us—not just the act of sex, but the whole realm of sexuality, including intimacy, procreation, sexual pleasure, and loving relationships. The Buddha saw sexual energy as the strongest of all the energies we experience, and perhaps the most difficult to relate to skillfully. He said that if there were another energy as powerful as the lust for sex, no one would ever get enlightened, including himself. That very power is what enables us to deal with the energy of sexuality and work with it skillfully: the energies of aversion, hatred, and delusion simply aren't as powerful as the desire for sex, and thus they can be overcome. While our species' desire to procreate—an offshoot of our survival instinct—may not be conscious, it is present in all of us on a cellular level.

We love sex and we often fall in romantic love with our sex partners. Of course this is not always true—indeed, a lot of people have a lot of sex without feelings of romantic love—but for the sake of this section, I will write as though love and sex were connected for most of us, most of the time. I understand that sex and love are complex and often separate issues, and I know that conflating them will not serve everyone's needs. But I also know that, for almost everyone, sex and love will overlap at times in life. I don't want to say that you always have to be in love to have sex, or that you will fall in love with everyone that you have sex with, or even that it's *better* to be in love with your sex partners. I'm not trying to make any moral judgments or ethical rules. I'm just trying to address the experience that we all have at one time or another, or over and over, of being intoxicated by the impermanent experience of romantic love.

The pleasure and intimacy that sexuality provides create such a wonderful delusion of security and happiness that we tend to call it love. In romantic love we feel embraced and seen and appreciated. Sex is the primary bond in romantic love, the mutual pleasure that is experienced through giving and receiving sexual acts.

Romantic love is almost always conditional and impermanent, however. To be in love is wonderful—it is a great joy to experience romantic love—but such love inevitably ends. Even in an ongoing romantic relationship there are times when the desires of the partners aren't in harmony—the old "I'm not in the mood." And even in an absolute dream relationship, one where you fall in love and live happily ever after, someone eventually dies first, and the other is left with great sorrow: "happily ever after" inevitably ends in either your death or the loss of your life partner.

Attachment seems to be inherent in romantic relationships, and therein lies the rub. The goal of unconditional/unattached interaction is put to the test once sex enters the picture. Human beings naturally get attached to the pleasure of sexual intimacy—an intimacy that involves not just the physical pleasure of sex, as noted above, but also feelings of security and safety. Even when one of the partners is unattached—or, more likely, emotionally unavailable—the other will often cling to the idea that the unattached partner will change, and thus the clinger creates great suffering for him- or herself.

The problem of attachment isn't particular to romantic love, of course. Our lack of acceptance of impermanence gets us into all kinds of trouble, as we've seen. We don't like things to change, whatever the arena. But that attachment is a special problem with romantic love, because sexual desire and sexual fulfillment are natural and beautiful and pleasurable. *Of course* we want the pleasure of sex and love and intimacy. But we don't want the experience to change or end, nor do we want our beloved partner to change (or, in the case of misalignment, we *do* want him or her to change). We don't want to understand or accept the fact that everyone and everything is going to change in their own way and on their own time schedule. For instance, I've known several couples who, when they got together as young adults, shared a mutual understanding that neither of them wanted kids. But as they grew older, things changed: one of them began to want children. This sort of evolution creates a great dilemma for couples who are still very much in love with each other. The change that has taken place is either a deal-breaker or, at the very least, a great barrier to get through. In the case of my friends, some of the couples broke up; others stayed together, with the one who wanted children having to let go of that desire, or the one who *didn't* want them having to rise to the unwanted joys of parenting.

Sometimes people are fortunate enough in romantic love relationships to change at about the same pace and in the same direction; in other words, they change together. They come together and grow, and it seems to work out. Other people develop some level of unconditionality around the relationship and allow their partner to grow and change without feeling threatened. Most of us, though, succumb to the pervasive delusion that if something changes in us or in our partner, we are somehow to blame—or they are. We take change as betrayal. We move from "We used to have sex every night, and now we do it only once a week" to "You must not love me anymore." We take impermanence and change personally, as if they were somehow our fault (or our partner's). Often our reaction is to hold on, to grasp at the way things used to be, or to fall into the delusion that we can change our lover into the person we want him or her to be. We tend to get stuck in the way we want things to be rather than rest in the acceptance of the way things are.

The Buddha saw how challenging it is to be involved in sexual relationships without getting caught—without getting hooked or attached and inevitably experiencing suffering. His response was to prescribe an attitude of loving-kindness toward all living beings rather than to just one. He acknowledged the possibility of total liberation within sexual relationships but seemed to feel that it would be even more difficult to be free from suffering within sexual relationships than if one chose celibacy. Indeed, celibacy was what the Buddha practiced and prescribed to all who chose the monastic path. Celibacy is a viable option, certainly. We don't *need* to have sex, despite what our survival instinct tells us; we *choose* to.

Those of us who choose the path of sex and relationships rather than celibacy have our work cut out for us. For that reason, it is important that we take full responsibility for the fact that we are *choosing* to participate: we are not victims, we are not powerless—we are choosing an aspect of life that is challenging. For those of us who are spiritually minded, our sexual relationships become a key aspect of our dharma practice. The practice and goal is one of nonattachment. But remember that *non*attachment does not mean *de*tachment. *Detachment* means "separation from"; to detach is to pull away, to disengage. *Nonattachment,* on the other hand, is a fully engaged and connected experience of being in the middle of whatever is going on, without clinging to or trying to control it. In romantic relationships we do the dance of clinging / detaching / reconnecting / being lovingly connected (nonattached) / clinging / detaching . . . over and over. But the Buddhist practices of the heart help us to gain more and more ability to sustain the ideal of nonattached loving connectedness. And when we fail, as we surely will, we have the practice of forgiveness to help us let go more easily and to begin the dance again.

Chapter 8

THE METTA SUTTA

loving-kindness: the "high-way" to freedom

The Buddha was clear and precise about the human need and ability to free oneself so completely from attachment and aversion that only a loving heart would remain. This is a radical proposal, to be sure—but one that is not out of reach or unrealistic. It does *not* mean that we can't stay connected to our romantic and personal loving relationships. The awakened heart has room for it all. Of course, if your partners, friends, and family aren't also in the process of awakening, they may not like that you have as much love for the homeless guy on the street as you do for them!

The Buddha's most precise teaching on this aspect of our heart/mind is found in a discourse called the Metta Sutta.

Metta translates as "goodwill," "friendliness," "loving-kindness," or "unconditional love," depending on whom you ask. *Sutta* means "teaching." The Metta Sutta, then, is a teaching from the Buddha on love, kindness, goodwill, and unconditional friendliness. I would like to devote this next section to looking at the profound implications that this teaching holds for us.

Metta Sutta: The Buddha's Words on Loving-Kindness

This is what should be done by one who is skilled in goodness,
And who knows the path of peace:
Let them be able and upright,
Straightforward and gentle in speech.
Humble and not conceited,
Contented and easily satisfied.
Unburdened with duties and frugal in their ways.
Peaceful and calm, and wise and skillful,
Not proud and demanding in nature.
Let them not do the slightest thing that the wise would later reprove.
Wishing: In gladness and in safety,
May all beings be at ease.
Whatever living beings there may be;
Whether they are weak or strong, omitting none,
The great or the mighty, medium, short or small,
The seen and the unseen,
Those living near and far away,
Those born and to-be-born,

May all beings be at ease!
Let none deceive another,
Or despise any being in any state.
Let none through anger or ill will
Wish harm upon another.
Even as a mother protects with her life
Her child, her only child,
So with a boundless heart
Should one cherish all living beings:
Radiating kindness over the entire world—
Spreading upwards to the skies,
And downwards to the depths;
Outwards and unbounded,
Freed from hatred and ill will.
Whether standing or walking, seated or lying down
Free from drowsiness,
One should sustain this recollection.
This is said to be the sublime abiding.
By not holding to fixed views,
The pure-hearted one, having clarity of vision,
Being freed from all sense desires,
Is not born again into this world.

Let's examine each of these lines in depth:

This is what should be done by one who is skilled in goodness,
And who knows the path of peace.

I have always found this opening statement to be a little off-putting. If we already knew the path of peace and were skilled in goodness, why would we need to put so much effort into meditation? So I tend to hear these words as meaning, "This is what should be done by those who *wish to be* skilled in goodness and who *wish to know* the path of peace." In other words, I hear the statement as a proclamation of where I am *heading*. It says to me that if I follow this way, it will lead to my becoming skilled in goodness and to knowing the path of peace. Sounds good to me. If "skilled in goodness" means that I will not experience or cause suffering anymore, sign me up. And if knowing peace means that I will be at ease in any circumstance, bring it on. I'm ready to gain some skills and knowledge!

Let them be able and upright.

Now the instructions begin, but what does it mean to be able and upright? It is my understanding that *all* beings are able to love, to awaken, and to know peace. I hear this instruction as meaning, "We have to show up for the hard work that lies ahead." It reminds me of an Italian gangster vouching for his friend, saying, "He's a stand-up guy; he's totally able and upright." A stand-up guy or gal is one with integrity, someone who is trustworthy and willing to do what needs to be done for "the family." The *sangha* (or community) of meditators is not unlike a Mafia family in this respect. Are you gonna be true to the *sangha*? And act with integrity for the cause of liberation?

Being upright may also have something to do with meditation posture—sitting upright, training the heart and mind in goodness and peace.

Straightforward and gentle in speech

The instruction to be "straightforward and gentle in speech" is much clearer. To live our life from a place of love, we have to be wise and careful with our communications. Being straightforward means exhibiting honesty, and certainly speaking the truth is an integral part of being loving. However, honesty can be either gentle or brutal. The Buddha encourages us toward gentleness. This doesn't mean we have to whisper all the time; it doesn't mean we have to adopt a really soft tone of voice that sounds like we're on Quaaludes. No, it's a practical suggestion to check out our intention: Is what we are about to say coming from a place of love—a gentle and appropriate place—or are we caught up in some bullshit and speaking from a place of ill will, dishonesty, or selfishness? As you may have noticed from my use of the term *bullshit* in the previous sentence, I don't believe that swearing is outside the realm of being straightforward and gentle. As a matter of fact, I think that *not* swearing when strong words are called for can be a form of dishonesty, another spiritual mask we put on, like the self-consciously soothing Quaalude voice. As a stand-up guy or gal, we are asked to be real. Not to play some fake-ass spiritual make-believe, but to source our communication from the heart.

Humble and not conceited

Humility is at the core of the path of love. The more loving and wise we become, the more the ego will want to lay claim to the experiences of wisdom. Humility is not a state of ego-lessness; it is a wise relationship to the ego. Humility does not mean that conceit doesn't arise in the mind; it means that conceit is met with the wisdom of not taking the inflation personally. Usually when we are feeling inflated and conceited, we believe the ego's insistence that we are better or worse than others. Humility is a practice that allows us to override that insistence and arrive at a wise relationship to the ego. It takes constant vigilance, because the mind is constantly creating (and attempting to give permanence to) a self out of that aspect of our experience that we call *ego*, constantly creating conceit.

Conceit is both inflation and deflation of the sense of self, though only the former usage is common. Conceit is what results when we believe the internal dialogue—believe the ego's aforementioned insistence that we are better or worse than others—and identify with that comparative evaluation as who we are. When the inner dialogue is imbalanced toward an inflated sense of who we are, it's called *self-centeredness* or *ego-inflation*. When the inner dialogue is imbalanced toward a deflated sense of self, it's called *self-doubt, low self-esteem,* or *self-hatred.* In other words, self-doubt and self-hatred are forms of conceit. Conceit is not so much about what has arisen in the mind regarding who we are, as it is about the extent to which we allow those thoughts to define who we are. Humility means humbly accepting that we are worthy of love and kindness, that we have everything we need to be happy right here inside of us. Not being conceited means understanding that ego trips—whether inflated or deflated—are not worth taking personally. Don't fall into Mara's trap of believing all of what the mind experiences!

Contented and easily satisfied

Being contented and easily satisfied feels like a tall order. I can hear it as a practice that works toward an acceptance of what is offered. However, I believe that it's pointing toward something much deeper than a begrudging acceptance of the subpar circumstances of life. To be contented means to truly be fulfilled by what is happening, by the food that is served, by the service that is offered, by the weather, by the relationships we are in, by the work that we do—contented with *what is*. This is another place where I wish the Buddha had stated the point more actively: as "*striving to be* contented and easily satisfied." Contentment and satisfaction are processes rather than permanent states of being; they are among the desired outcomes of our dharma practice, but they are also moment-to-moment choices, every day. "Can I accept and be satisfied with this moment as it is?" Honesty is necessary here. Sometimes the answer is yes; often the answer is that we're not quite there yet. We're still caught up in our preferences. But the key is to understand that it is possible to be easily satisfied, to know the happiness of accepting our life as it is, while still working toward less suffering and more freedom.

Unburdened with duties and frugal in their ways

Notice that this does not say "*free* from duties"; rather, it states that the wise do not *feel burdened* by their duties. We all have our duties—our professional duties, our household or familial duties, our community or social duties. Let's say, for instance, that you are called upon for jury duty. Everybody resents jury duty, with its interruption of routine and its pitiful remuneration. But the next time you're summoned, try to show up with an attitude of kindness and feel unburdened by the responsibility. Gauge how that changes the experience.

We are always doing *something*. Sometimes our tasks are pleasant; sometimes they are unpleasant. On the path of loving-kindness, it is important to remember that the unpleasant duties are not a burden, but just another opportunity for kindness and compassion. The balance that we seek can be found only through showing up in equal integrity, whether the duty is enjoyable or not. The outcome of this virtue is that we are no longer doing what needs to be done begrudgingly: we show up for our duties and perform them without complaint or resentment.

Looking at the other half of the phrase, being frugal means being balanced and appropriate in the ways we spend our time, energy, and money. It does not mean being uptight or rigid about expenditures; rather, it simply means spending the amount of time, energy, or resources each given situation demands—but no more. It means not going overboard, not getting lost in gluttony and excess.

There is an important implication here for our meditative training. As in all things, in meditation we need to learn to be balanced, appropriate, and frugal. We don't want to overextend ourselves, to become *excessive* in our striving for freedom. At times over the years I have become imbalanced in my life by putting too much time and energy into my meditation practice and consequently ignoring some of my other duties and responsibilities, such as my physical health or my financial well-being. I have come to understand that to be frugal means to give equal attention to *each* area of my life. It has become clear to me that, rather than meditating all day every day, I need to make tasks such as exercising, eating right, and balancing my checkbook part of my daily duties, to be performed in wise and frugal ways.

Peaceful and calm

Becoming peaceful and calm is a goal that most people would readily affirm. However, it is important to remember that being peaceful as an individual does not mean that life is peaceful or that the world is at peace. Peacefulness is not the absence of external difficulties or conflict. Instead, it is an internal relationship to whatever is happening, whether it is pleasant, painful, or neutral. Most of us carry some deep delusions about what it means to be peaceful. We cling to a concept of peace as a state of pleasantness, where nothing is difficult or painful or challenging. This idea of peace must be replaced by the reality that you will *never* create a world that has no difficulties; your only hope is to create a relationship to the sorrow and joy in this world that is in harmony with reality. Not suffering about suffering is being at peace with suffering. Not grasping at nongrasping is being at peace with grasping.

The calm of metta is also that of being at ease in the midst of what is. Not a calmness that means the placid lake is unmoving, but a calmness of riding the crashing waves of *samsara*, the Buddhist notion of the sea of existence, without becoming seasick. The practice here is of accepting what is and responding in a calm and peaceful manner. Again, calm is not the absence of challenging circumstances; it refers to a relaxed and calm response to whatever is happening.

Wise and skillful

I like that wise and skillful are grouped together here. To be wise means to know reality. From this perspective it could be as simple as having insight into impermanence, the truth of suffering and not-self. But to *know* what's going on and to be *skillful in relationship to* what's going on are two different things. For instance, we may have some wisdom into how our aversion to pain causes us a lot of unnecessary suffering, but we may not yet be skillful enough to always (or even often) replace the aversive reaction with the compassionate response that dharma practice calls for. To be skillful means to meet each experience with the appropriate response. In relationship to pain the skillful response is always compassion; in relationship to pleasure the skillful response is always appreciative nonclinging; in response to a neutral feeling the skillful response is just to let it be.

As important as wisdom is, it needs to be followed up with skillful actions. As was suggested above, we often develop an intellectually wise understanding of things before we develop consistently skillful actions. Kindness, for example, is always skillful, but it doesn't always mean being nice. Sometimes the skillful use of kindness requires that we enforce a firm boundary, that we in fact *stop* being outwardly nice and, from an internal place of kindness, act in a stern and serious way. On the other hand, compassion is *not* always a skillful response. Compassion is called for only in response to pain. If the experience is pleasurable, then compassion is uncalled for. Over the years of your meditative practice, you will gradually become more and more wise and more and more skillful.

Not proud and demanding in nature

This instruction not to be proud or demanding reaffirms the earlier references to humility and acceptance. Avoiding pride is a great test for those following the Buddha's dharma when we start to feel like we've made serious progress on the path. To what extent do we allow the ego to take that progress personally? How much does spiritual pride begin to be another source of suffering in our lives (or, more likely, in the lives of the people who have to fit in the same room with us and our big egos)? I'm very fond of watching spiritual teachers, looking for these signs. If a teacher seems to be overly prideful or demanding, I begin to question his or her wisdom and skill. Many times over the years, I've had the experience of meeting spiritual teachers whom I admired based on their books or public lectures, and being disappointed, in person, by the way they seemed to be overly demanding of my efforts, attention, or respect. Now, this isn't to say that spiritual teachers can't have preferences. It's fine to know what you want and to ask for it. The practice here is not to make a problem out of not always getting what we want.

Pride can be a perfectly natural and healthy response to some situations—a job well done, a major accomplishment—but there is a healthy way to feel proud of ourselves or others. Notice that the Buddha added the words "demanding *in nature*." I hear this as a warning: it is okay to experience pride now and then and to ask for what you want; just don't let it become your nature to be always demanding things as you wish them to be.

Let them not do the slightest thing that the wise would later reprove.

This advice could save your life, or at least your karma. When you are about to do something that you suspect may be questionable in intention, reflect on what a wise being would think of the action. I find it useful to bring to mind specific people who I believe are wise. I often think of one of my two main teachers, Jack Kornfield and Ajahn Amaro. Sometimes I even reflect on what the Buddha would say about my actions. What would Buddha do? WWBD? This simple reflection can help us to live with more integrity. When we ask ourselves if the wise would approve or disapprove, we usually can intuit fairly quickly the answer, and therefore get a sense of whether we are acting in integrity with the wisdom that we claim to be trying to cultivate.

Be careful, though: I've often seen myself look for loopholes in this practice, so I know what an easy trap it is. For instance, I often catch myself calculating *which* wise person to reflect on based on the situation. If the situation has anything to do with sex or money, I probably wouldn't think about Ajahn Amaro, because he is a monk and has vowed to live a life of celibacy and nonparticipation with money. I would more likely think about and perhaps even ask Jack Kornfield, since as a lay teacher he is more likely to give me an answer that I would like. Having repeatedly caught myself looking for the easy way out, I've taken to putting myself and my actions under the scrutiny of both monastic and lay teachers. What would the monks think? What would my fellow teachers at the Spirit Rock Meditation Center think? And what would my students think?

Something important to remember here is that there will always be both praise and blame for every course of action. In the Metta Sutta, the Buddha specifies that we should think of "the wise." I take this to mean "the fully enlightened ones." And since none of our current teachers seem to be fully enlightened, we have to accept that at times we will be judged and reproved by people's ignorance rather than their wisdom.

But just imagine the freedom that comes from living in a way that is blameless in the eyes of the wise! Sure, you might have to give up some of your indulgences, but the happiness of blamelessness is a greater joy than all the temporary fixes in this world. The happiness of blamelessness allows us to live with confidence and security that we are living a wise life. When we are blameless in the eyes of the wise, we have nothing to regret and nothing to make amends for.

> *Wishing: In gladness and in safety,*
> *May all beings be at ease.*

This is the part of the Metta Sutta where the actual meditation instructions begin: we are instructed to wish for all beings to be at ease. But to wish "in gladness and in safety"—what does that mean? I hear that as an instruction to come from a place of gratitude and a willingness to protect. Although meditation practice based on this instruction often takes the form of wishing, "May all beings be safe and protected from harm," followed by "May all beings be at ease," I don't use the first line. I prefer not to think about safety in that sense, because I don't want to be training my heart and mind to wish for something that is not possible. Although it is possible for people to be at ease even in the most painful or difficult situations, I don't believe that there will ever come a time when everyone is safe and protected from harm. We live in a world that is *unsafe,* filled with ignorance and hatred. People are constantly harming each other; animals are constantly killing each other. There is no safety, but there is certainly a way to be at ease in the midst of the danger—a safety of the heart/mind, if you will.

Of course, it is a beautiful and noble wish to ask for physical safety and protection for all beings, and perhaps the repetition of such unattainable wishes is good for our own mind/heart; still, to me it has always felt a bit dishonest to wish for something that I believe is impossible.

Another phrase that often gets added on here is "May all beings be happy." Although the Buddha's actual instruction was only to wish for "ease," perhaps being at ease and being happy are closely connected. But if we're going to wish for happiness, I think it is very important to have a realistic definition of what real happiness is.

Most people have a deep confusion about what it means to be happy. The general idea seems to be that we're happy when everything is going the way we want it to, which almost always means that things feel good and pleasurable. Well, if our definition of happiness is "experiencing that which is pleasurable," we are going to be disappointed a lot of the time. Using that definition, it would be impossible to be happy all of the time, because it is impossible to sustain pleasure all of the time. From a Buddhist perspective, though, it *is* possible to be happy all of the time. That's because for the Buddhist, the definition of happiness isn't tied to pleasure; it's closer to "ease" or "acceptance" or "contentment." So if you are wishing for happiness for yourself or others, I urge you to make sure you have a realistic understanding of what is possible.

As the next line will show us, we are instructed here to include everyone in our meditative repetition of our "ease" wishes. Traditionally this is done systematically, by having categories of people toward whom we send loving-kindness in our meditations. We often begin with ourselves and move on to sending love to the people who have been kind and beneficent to us. Then we expand to people we're neutral toward and friends and family about whom we have mixed feelings. Finally, we include the difficult people in our lives, and even our enemies, before expanding the field of loving intentions out to all beings everywhere—all of the countless beings we don't know or have contact with.

The question will often arise, Who or what is it that we are wishing to? Is this some kind of Buddhist *prayer*? The answer is yes, perhaps this *is* the Buddhist equivalent of prayer, but rather than asking for happiness and peace from an external source of spiritual power, we are training the heart/mind. The repetition of the loving-kindness phrases begins to uncover the heart's innate loving and kindness. Through this practice of training the heart/mind to respond with love, and with the understanding that all beings are ultimately the same, we begin spreading love outward and wishing happiness for all others. The outcome of long-term loving-kindness meditation is the experience of friendliness toward all beings. Our hearts open to the joy and suffering of all people as we gain the ability to care and to love without being overwhelmed by the vastness of the world.

> *Whatever living beings there may be;*
> *Whether they are weak or strong, omitting none,*
> *The great or the mighty, medium, short or small,*
> *The seen and the unseen,*

Those living near and far away,
Those born and to-be-born,
May all beings be at ease!

The key phrases here are "omitting none" and "May all beings be at ease." The Buddha is clear that we are to break our small-mindedness about whom to love and whom not to love. The first thing I would like to point out is that you yourself are included in the "all"! Too often we hear Buddhist presentations of loving-kindness or compassion stated as "toward others." The Buddha talks about "*all* living beings," though—and you are just as worthy of your love as everyone else.

The Buddha reminds us that *all* includes both the weak and the strong. One of the most obvious connotations of "weak or strong" is that group which includes both the oppressors and the oppressed in this world. This is an incredibly challenging task: we are asked to see deeply enough into the hearts of the oppressors—including the homophobes, racists, enemies of the environment, and warmongers—that we can meet them with a wish for their ease and well-being. That runs contrary to our habitual tendency of meeting ignorance and oppression with aversion and hatred. Forgiveness is needed in order to proceed any further with metta practice. And as we discussed in a previous chapter, forgiveness is a process of meeting pain with compassion. Forgiveness and mercy, if we can learn to extend them to others, end much of the suffering in our lives. Well, we are asked here to be open to sending these kind wishes to everyone—even the most difficult to love.

The great, the mighty, the medium, the short or small—okay, we get it: everyone! With the great I think of whales, elephants, and all of the other incredibly large beings. The mighty could be predators such as sharks, lions, and warlords. The medium could be average humans. The short could be cats, dogs, birds, and so on. And the small could be bugs, insects, and other critters down to the tiniest microbes. Of course, this is not an exhaustive list of living beings, just a very cursory overview. What is very clear from these descriptors—great, mighty, etc.—is that the Buddha is talking about all human beings, all mammals, all fish and creatures of the sea, all birds, all insects, all, all, *all* . . .

But wait, there's more. Not just the living beings visible to the human eye or microscope. Don't forget "the seen and the unseen." Here we are being asked to open our minds to the possibility of living beings in realms that are not knowable by ordinary human consciousness. This may include not only earthworms (which we do not see without digging) but also spirits, ghosts, devas, and the gods themselves. (As a side note, if there are gods, or a god, it is clear that they are deeply in need of some kindness and love. Perhaps with a good dose of metta, the god of theistic religions would not be so wrathful, destructive, judgmental, and jealous.)

We are also reminded to spread metta toward those "living near and far away." It is very important that we include those out of sight and out of mind. For some, those living near are easier to feel kindness toward: because we see and interact with them, we can more easily understand their pain and sorrow, and thus perhaps more easily forgive them. On the other hand, the ones we know and are near to can also pose a great challenge, especially if their suffering and confusion affect us directly. In that sense, those who are far away can be easier to forgive and therefore to love—although it can be difficult to generate kind feelings toward the unknown. But the more we do so, the more we will have an attitude of kindness toward *each* new person we encounter. It becomes a feeling of "I've never met you before, but I've been praying for your well-being, so it's nice to finally meet you."

"Those born and to-be-born"—again the Buddha is covering all the bases here. Let's not forget all the millions of beings who are to be born *today*.

Let none deceive another.

This is a clear reference to the necessity of honesty. Without the ethical boundaries of integrity and honesty in speech and actions, we will certainly never be able to experience the ease and well-being of loving-kindness. With dishonesty comes fear, and with fear come discomfort and uneasiness. One of the ways that metta is talked about is "having an open heart"—a heart of wisdom and compassion, a heart of love and kindness. While it is impossible to lie with an open heart, dishonesty closes the heart: when we deceive another or ourselves, we shut down a part of our heart.

On the Buddhist path, we don't have to be perfect—we don't even have to be kind all of the time—but we do have to be honest. Without honesty we are dead in the water. As with so much of life, becoming honest is a process. In my own case it took me a few years to learn how to tell others the truth all of the time, and I still wrestle with occasional self-deception. My pre-dharma life was so filled with dishonesty that at times I didn't know the truth from the deceptions I had fabricated. For instance, as a kid I lied about being at punk shows in San Francisco, at the legendary Mabuhay Gardens, although the "Mab" had closed in the mideighties, before I was old enough to attend a show there. But I had collected some of the fliers and had seen some videos of bands playing there. Supported by that "evidence," the lies I told about having been there were so persuasive that at times even I believed them.

Honesty must become our practice and priority. It wasn't until I could tell the truth all of the time, until I stopped deceiving anyone, that I really began to feel at ease in my own skin. With the humility of being honest even when it made me look bad came the freedom of having nothing to hide.

Or despise any being in any state

Although there is nowhere in the original teachings of the Buddha where he explicitly says to forgive, this is one of the closest and clearest statements about the need for forgiveness. In order not to despise any being in any state, we are going to have a lot of forgiving to do. Our heart/mind is wired to despise. As noted earlier, we are born with a hatred of pain in every aspect of our being. As we grow up and our hearts and minds mature, the hatred of pain becomes resentment and spite toward all people, places, and things that have hurt us in the past. Because despising is a built-in part of the untrained mind, this is not a discipline that can be undertaken as a simple choice: "Hmm, okay, I will simply not resent anyone anymore." Nope, it doesn't work like that. Resentments are the habitual reactions of the self-protective survival instinct of our species. I believe that this is part of what the Buddha was referring to when he stated that the path goes "against the stream" (the subject of my previous book, titled with that phrase). The stream flows in the direction of despising lots of beings in lots of states. Perhaps with enlightenment comes an easy and clear ability to let go of all the pain of our past, but for the rest of us—those of us still struggling with resentments—we are going to have to intentionally trudge the path and practice forgiveness.

This path of becoming loving, of having an open heart and free mind, is getting more and more radical. First we're supposed to wish for our enemies to be at ease; now it sounds like we're not allowed even to *have* enemies. Shit, who will I be without any resentments? And what about my poor nemeses? Who will they be if I deprive them of an enemy?

Let none through anger or ill will
Wish harm upon another.

Clearly, wishing harm upon people is not congruent with wishing for all beings to be at ease. I like that this instruction isn't saying that anger and ill will won't arise, but simply that we can come to a place of not acting or even wishing from these negative emotions. But the ultimate goal of this statement is that we can come to a place of deep enough love and kindness that we will no longer want to hurt any living being. It is a lofty aspiration, to be sure. When we are injured or even just offended, our instinct is to want to injure in return. "You hurt me; I hurt you." Or, "You hurt someone I love; I wish harm upon you." Or, "You do something that I don't like to people I don't even know, and I *still* hate you." Freedom from this cycle of judgment, ill will, and the wish to harm is a radical departure from how the masses of people—even spiritual and religious people—tend to function. The wisdom that is needed here is that *all* beings are suffering; *all* oppression and harm come from a place of ignorance. Almost all of the time, the person whom we are wishing harm upon is already deeply suffering. Given that, our reactive wish to harm, the result of a merciless ignorance within us, makes us act like the schoolyard bully picking on a severely disabled child. The people that you want to harm are already severely disabled. You may not see their handicaps, but that's most likely because you haven't been paying very close attention. No one ever oppresses, suppresses, or intentionally injures another out of wisdom; all of the ways we cause harm come from ignorance. So when we meet ignorance with wishes for harm to come to the ignorant, we are joining in the cycle of ignorance. Love would tell us to meet ignorance with genuine compassion and understanding. As the Buddha said, "Hatred will never cease by hatred; by love alone does hatred cease."

Even as a mother protects with her life
Her child, her only child,
So with a boundless heart
Should one cherish all living beings.

This is a powerful image of the kind of complete commitment that is required on the path of loving-kindness. As a parent I am fully aware of the implications of this instruction. I am constantly vigilant about protecting my daughter from harm. It is so easy and natural to care deeply for our own children, but to open our hearts enough to cherish and protect all living beings in an equal way sounds almost impossible. At this point in my life I relate to this instruction the way I relate to Zen Buddhism's bodhisattva vow, which in part says something like "Suffering is endless; I vow to end it all. Beings are numberless; I vow to save them all." However we put it, it is an incredibly noble and totally impossible task. While I don't think that I can truly cherish and protect all living beings the way a good mother loves, cherishes, and protects her only child, I am willing to strive for that kind of loving relationship to all living beings.

As with many of the lines in the Metta Sutta, the perfections that are pointed to are noble goals, and the transformative effect that the repetition of such goals has on our heart and mind is perhaps just as important as the goals themselves. I can't tell you how many times I've been walking down the street and, when the above-quoted lines have come into my mind, experienced a complete change in my attitude toward everyone I pass. When we remember to see others through the eyes of a loving mother, we smile more easily, are generous more readily, and forgive more quickly.

This may be the root of the Tibetan Buddhist practice of seeing each person we encounter as having been our mother in a past life. The Tibetans have adopted teachings which say that we are all constantly reincarnating, and indeed have been doing so for so long that when we meet someone, we've already been connected to that person for countless incarnations. And not just connected, but related, having actually parented each other, having actually given birth to each other. Next time you are experiencing conflict with someone—say, the guy who just stole your parking place or cut you off in traffic—reflect that although that person is being selfish and inconsiderate at this moment, in this lifetime, in a past lifetime he or she was incredibly generous, breastfeeding you and loving you unconditionally. It may be easier, with that in mind, to say, "Go ahead and take the spot, Mom."

While that outlook may or may not be true in a literal sense, it is incredibly useful to train our hearts and minds to love in such a spacious and generous way. Likewise, attempting to love each being as though he or she were our child, as the Buddha suggests in the above-quoted instruction, is a great practice. Know what I mean, kiddo?

Radiating kindness over the entire world—
Spreading upwards to the skies,
And downwards to the depths;
Outwards and unbounded.

Loving-kindness is the experience of having a friendly and loving relationship toward ourselves as well as all others. The experience of sending loving-kindness toward ourselves is perhaps as simple as bringing a friendly attitude to our minds and bodies. Typically, we tend to judge ourselves and be quite critical and harsh in our self-assessments, identifying with the negative thoughts and feelings that arise in our minds. Being loving and kind isn't our normal habit, so training the heart/mind to be kind is a great task. Mindfulness brings the mind's negative habits into awareness. Loving-kindness meditation is a way of creating new, more positive habits. As we see how much difficulty we create for ourselves and begin to respond with compassion, we come to understand that ultimately we want nothing more than to be free from the causes of suffering and confusion. As we gain insight into the impersonal nature of the thinking mind and feeling body, we come to understand that *all* beings would like this same freedom—a liberated heart that we might call happiness.

Radiating loving-kindness over the entire world is the heart/mind's response of wishing such freedom and happiness for ourselves and all others. The process begins with a simple practice of setting intentions—that is, by wishing that we might be happy, at ease, and free from suffering. We don't have to be sincere in the beginning; it's okay to start where we are. It may take months or even years before we are able to sincerely connect with a feeling of loving-kindness toward all living beings. Especially given that, as I mentioned earlier, there's probably going to be a good amount of forgiveness to be done in order to

include the difficult people. But it also takes time to really understand that we're all the same, all having a similarly difficult
time of incarnation. When we begin to truly love ourselves,
when we truly forgive ourselves, we can more and more easily
love and forgive others. Sending love to strangers across the
world will become easier as we gradually realize that all beings
are worthy of kindness, all beings deserve love.

Freed from hatred and ill will

This line says that, if you've made it this far, love and kindness will become so completely all-encompassing that you will
have been freed from hatred and ill will. My own perspective
is that the best we can hope for is freedom from *becoming identified with* these feelings, or perhaps the freedom from *acting out of*
anger or ill will. It does not ring true to me that we will come
to a place where anger will no longer arise. It seems clear that
anger is a fairly primal and built-in aspect of our heart/mind. It
makes sense that we get better and better at meeting pain with
compassion and mercy. It makes sense that we no longer want
to hurt anyone. But I'm not buying that these feeling will be
wiped clean from our minds or hearts.

As I've said in earlier chapters, the Buddha referred to his
own hatred and ill will as the opponent Mara; and even after
enlightenment, Mara persisted in the Buddha's heart/mind.
But when Mara did arise, the Buddha always met his opponent with wise and compassionate awareness, saying, "I see
you, Mara." To me this means that when ill will arose for the

Buddha, he had a wise relationship to that ill will; he paid attention to it. "I see you, ill will; I see you, hatred," and in the seeing is the freedom. When we relate to our difficult emotions—when we see them clearly and thus respond wisely—we are freed from the suffering that they usually cause.

Whether standing or walking, seated or lying down

Although very often the formal practice of metta is done as a silent, seated meditation, it's clear from the above statement that it can and should be brought into all postures and activities. As we have already discussed, metta is not a rarified or temporary experience to be achieved only during intensive meditation. On the contrary, metta is a state of mind and a response of the heart. And as this commentary on the Metta Sutta has highlighted, metta is not just one thing but many, many different yet connected practices. Metta includes humility, integrity, forgiveness, kindness, generosity, love, acceptance, altruism, and honesty. Metta is an intention of all-around friendliness that is meant to be cultivated, practiced, and lived from. So it makes sense, of course, that it is not dependent on any certain posture or activity, but that we want to bring these wise intentions into all of our activities. So when we are walking down the street, we are encouraged to radiate loving-kindness to each being we pass. While we are sitting on the train or bus, we are including everyone in our kind wishes. No matter where we are or what we are doing, metta is always a good idea.

That having been said, I do encourage a regular and disciplined sitting meditation practice of metta (as outlined at the end of this chapter). There is something powerful that happens when we are focused and still, when there are no outward distractions and the mind can settle on the gentle repetition of the metta phrases. So I encourage both a formal and an informal approach: create a daily sitting meditation practice, but also, throughout the activities of your day, repeat the relevant phrases and reflect on the qualities of humility, integrity, forgiveness, kindness, generosity, love, acceptance, altruism, and honesty.

Free from drowsiness,
One should sustain this recollection.

Drowsiness is one of the things that the Buddha feels hinders our progress along the path. When we are drowsy (or slothful or spaced out—however you want to put it), we are not fully mindful and present, which makes it difficult to be intentional. Of course, the Buddha is not saying that we should never be sleepy, just that it is important to be alert and intentional. In order to sustain this intentional way of being, thinking, and acting, it is important to get enough sleep, eat healthy food, drink plenty of water, and get enough exercise. All of these factors affect our mind-state. In short, in order to be alert and fully present in our body, it is necessary to have a balanced health regimen.

This is said to be the sublime abiding.

"The sublime abiding" is another way of saying "the happiest place to be" or "an enlightened way of being." And it makes perfect sense: if we can live in a way that is humble, honest, completely free from resentments, radiating kindness with the sincere wish that all living beings be at ease, happy, and free from suffering, then of course we are going to be living in a state of happiness ourselves. This is also an important reminder that training our heart, mind, and body to live in accordance with metta does not create a whole world of happiness. Our wishes do not magically end suffering *for others;* the metta practice is about our *personal* transformation. Through a thorough training in metta—through doing "what should be done by one who is skilled in goodness, and who knows the path of peace"—we find a sublime abiding, a cool place to hang out. An internal place of ease and well-being is the outcome of metta. And of course our awakening, our transformation, does have a very, *very* positive effect on the world. To be one less person who is acting out of ignorance and ill will is a great offering to all beings. To be someone who sincerely wishes wellness and ease to everyone she or he meets is a great service and is incredibly inspiring.

So yes, metta *does* create positive change in the world, but it is only through personal, internal transformation that such change takes place.

By not holding to fixed views

"Not holding to fixed views" has several connotations here. It is a direct instruction: "Don't get attached to any perspective—not even metta," along with "Let go of your old views and ideas about what happiness is." It is also a foundation for all of the forgiveness that we have been asked to do, because if we hold to fixed views about people, we will never be able to forgive. Forgiveness is, in effect, a change in the way we view people, a move from keeping people tied to their past actions, to releasing them from that identity and beginning to view them as an unfolding process. This allows the possibility of letting go—and not just of our former, fixed views, but also of our resentments—enabling us to have mercy and meet others with kindness.

Not holding to fixed views is also a way that the Buddha continues to encourage us toward a genuine humility and open-mindedness. He once said that it seemed one of the ways that spiritually minded people suffer most is by getting attached to their views—in other words, that holding to fixed views is a great trap for many. So here we have another echo of the wisdom of nonattachment.

The pure-hearted one

At its core, I see the practice of metta as a process of purifying the heart. When we come to Buddhist practice, our hearts are polluted with resentments, anger, fear, judgments, demands, lusts, and ignorance. The practice of metta slowly transforms our hearts, stirring up all of the impurities, bringing all of the muck to the surface, where it can be healed. Metta heals the heart/mind: as it transforms the mind, it leaves us with a "pure heart." We become the "pure-hearted one" that the Buddha speaks of.

This line reminds us that we have always had metta as a heart-quality, but it has become so badly obscured by our instinctual and conditioned ignorance that we have lost touch with it. Now we return to a lost aspect of ourselves; now we recover our heart, our true heart, our pure-heartedness.

Having clarity of vision

Like the above statement about becoming pure-hearted, this line about having clarity of vision is connected to the outcome of intentional and long-term metta practice. We begin metta blind to some of our long-held confusions, resentments, fears, and small-mindedness. But through months and years of practicing humility, training the heart to respond with forgiveness, and wishing for happiness, ease, and freedom for all living beings, we begin to see reality more and more clearly. If you're not at that stage yet, don't be discouraged. At some point in the process, you may feel as if you're waking up from a bad dream. Or, when the freedom of heart and clarity of vision arise in your mind and body, you may feel like you finally got the right eyeglasses, finally were given the right optical prescription. Or perhaps it will feel more like you've been wearing glasses you never needed, your vision having been blurred all of these years unnecessarily. Metta allows us to remove the old perspectives and to have a clear view of the world.

Being freed from all sense desires

As with the first line in the Metta Sutta, I would have to
rewrite this one. To me it should read, "Being freed from *attachment to satisfying* all sense desires" or "Being freed from *all
craving for* sense desires." I have never believed that we can be
free from sense desires themselves. It is simply not possible. If
we are alive in a human body, we are going to have the experience of sense desires. I suspect that the above-quoted wording
is just a bad translation of the Buddha's teaching, because in
the second noble truth (listed in the Appendix with its fellow
truths) the Buddha makes a clear distinction between "craving"
and "desire." Desire is natural and healthy, and a necessary
aspect of the human experience, he says. The cause of suffering
is clearly not desire itself, but an extreme version of desire that
we call *craving, clinging,* and/or *attachment.*

So I encourage you to give up trying to be free from desire
and focus instead on becoming free from clinging. I'm sure you
will make much more progress.

Is not born again into this world

This last statement of the Metta Sutta can be taken a couple
different ways. It certainly can be taken literally, as follows: the
ultimate goal of the Buddha's path is freedom from the cycle of
rebirth, and the path of metta will culminate in that kind of
liberation. That is certainly a noble goal. If this interpretation
inspires you to practice for the end of rebirth, to no longer be

born again into this world, then it's fine to take this statement at face value.

Another way to understand this statement is to interpret "this world" as meaning "this world of suffering." "Birth" then refers to the way we often "take birth" by becoming identified with the experience of the mind and heart as who we are. When we take on the mind as our identity, we take birth *as the contents of the mind*—something we talked about earlier. When we learn to observe the mind as a conditioned and often confused aspect of our experience, then we are free *not* to be born over and over each moment into suffering. Thus the above statement could mean that we no longer take birth moment to moment in the world of ignorance and confusion in a way that causes suffering.

Making Sense of the Benefits of Metta

Reportedly, the Buddha said that there are eleven particular advantages to practicing metta:

1. You will sleep easily.

2. You will wake easily.

3. You will have pleasant dreams.

4. People will love you.

5. Animals and unseen beings will love you.

6. Unseen beings will protect you.

7. External dangers (such as fire, poison, and weapons) will not harm you.

8. Your face will be radiant.

9. Your mind will be serene.

10. You will die unconfused.

11. You will be reborn in happy realms.

With all of the Buddha's teachings, what is most important is that we can experience them directly. The dharma should make sense; it should be practical and applicable to our lives. When it comes to teachings like these eleven advantages, I suspect that some of what's said may be the fabrication of later idealists who wanted Buddhism to be mystical and magical rather than the practical path that the Buddha actually taught. But most of these promised advantages I find to be true in my own direct experience. I'll share with you here what makes most sense to me about these benefits, but ultimately you must trust yourself and make your own sense of such things.

The first three "promises" (sleep easily, wake easily, and have pleasant dreams) *do* make sense for me. As we heal our wounded heart and mind, as we forgive everyone everything, both the conscious and unconscious mind will rest with more ease. We will no longer be tormented by our petty resentments and fears that inhibit sleep; we will no longer suffer the restlessness of a loud mind and disturbed heart. Sleeping and waking will become the natural functions of the body that were always intended. Metta heals and soothes the heart/mind. And as the mind and heart are healed and purified, the unconscious mind in dream-states will also be healed and soothed.

The fourth and fifth promises (people and animals and unseen beings will love you) also make sense to me. The transformation that takes place through becoming a kind and loving person to all living beings enables people and animals to sense our kindness and thus feel safe. And with the feeling of being safe and protected from harm come feelings of love. It comes down to this: people who are genuinely kind and sincerely loving are easy to love. I think of the Dalai Lama in this way. Although we don't know him personally, his kindness and compassion shine through, and in response we love him. He is easy to love because he radiates metta. Some say that animals can sense fear; because metta ends neurotic fear, it makes sense that animals would also be able to sense the absence of fear and the presence of love and safety. All living beings want to feel safe, want to be free from the fear of being harmed. Animals love other animals that protect them from harm. With metta, we become the protectors, the allies, the stewards of the animal kingdom.

The sixth and seventh purported benefits of metta (being protected by unseen beings and from fire, poison, and guns) don't make much sense to me. I don't have any experience with unseen beings protecting me—but then again, how *would* I know since I wouldn't be able to see them when they were working their magic? With teachings like this, ones that get a little too mystical for me, my tendency is to set them aside in the "I don't know" category. Well, to be honest, my real tendency is not to have faith in anything that I can't experience directly. As far as metta protecting us from external harm, I am even more skeptical about that than about the angels. I suspect that this one may be a fabrication; in fact, I'm sure of it. We know that the Buddha died from ingesting poisoned food, so there's no way that this alleged benefit of metta could be true, or it would have protected him from the cause of his death. The only way that I can make any sense of "being protected from external dangers" is to see it as the capacity to experience the physical harms of fire, poison, and weapons without suffering at heart over the painful effects of these physical harms. Currently, that's a level of nonattachment that I can only imagine.

The eighth promise (a radiant face) seems true enough: with the freedom from resentments and fears, your face will become radiant with the joy of living a life based on kindness and love.

In the ninth benefit of metta the Buddha is quoted as promising that "your mind will be serene." This makes good sense on the level of having the serenity to relate to what arises in our minds with equanimity. But I worry about people getting the unrealistic idea that serenity means an absence of difficult emotions or conflicts. As with the line in the Metta Sutta where the Buddha advises us to be calm and peaceful, I hear it as an encouragement to relate to our experience and the experience of others with calm and peace. Whether joys or sorrows, if we relate to experiences in this skillful way, our heart/mind has the experience of serenity—even in the midst of, say, grief.

The tenth and eleventh promises are about death (unconfused) and rebirth (in a happy realm). Most people seem to die confused, feeling as if something has gone wrong. Even in the medical community, death is often treated as a failure. But with the understanding that arises through meditation, we begin to accept impermanence and death as simply the consequences of birth. Many people die still clinging to old resentments, guilt, and unfulfilled desires. Metta, the path of heartfulness, leads us in a direction of such integrity that we can die with a clear conscience. When we live a life that is free from anger, ill will, and fear, with the wisdom and compassion that are discovered along the way, death will no longer be so confusing.

I don't know much about rebirth. I'm not certain whether, in this context, the Buddha was being literal (talking about actually reincarnating) or metaphorical (pointing to the rebirth of allowing the old self to die, and being reborn in the next moment as a humble, easily contented, and loving person). I feel content to interpret the promise of rebirth in a happy realm to mean that in this lifetime metta will help us experience more happiness; and if there is a next lifetime, the work we do here and now will help with that one too.

Loving-Kindness Meditation Instructions

- Find a comfortable place to sit, and allow your attention to settle into the present-time experience of the

body. Relax any physical tension that is being held in
the body by softening the belly; relax the eyes and jaw
and allow your shoulders to naturally fall away from
the head.

- After a short period of settling into present-time
  awareness, begin to reflect on your deepest desire for
  happiness and freedom from suffering. Allow your
  heart's sincere longing for truth and well-being to come
  into consciousness.

- With each breath, breathe into the heart's center
  the acknowledgment of your wish to be free from
  harm, safe, and protected, and to experience love and
  kindness.

- Slowly begin to *offer yourself kind and friendly phrases* with
  the intention to uncover the heart's sometimes hidden
  loving and kind response. Your phrases can be as
  simple as the following:

  "May I be happy."

  "May I be at ease."

  "May I be free from suffering."

  If those phrases do not resonate with you, create your
  own words to meditate on. Find a few simple phrases
  that have a loving and kind intention, and slowly
  begin to offer these well-wishings to yourself.

- As you sit in meditation repeating these phrases in your
  mind, the attention may be drawn back (as in mindful-

ness meditation) into thinking about other things or resisting and judging the practice or your capacity for love. It takes a gentle and persistent effort to return to the next phrase each time the attention wanders:

"May I be happy."

Feel the breath and the body's response to each phrase.

"May I be at ease."

Notice where the mind goes with each phrase.

"May I be free from suffering."

Allow the mind and body to relax into the reverberations of each phrase.

Simply repeat these phrases over and over to yourself like a kind of mantra or statement of positive intention. But don't expect to instantly feel loving or kind as a result of this practice. Sometimes all we see is our lack of kindness and the judging mind's resistance. Simply acknowledge what is happening and continue to repeat the phrases, being as friendly and merciful with yourself as possible in the process.

- After a few minutes of sending these loving and kind phrases to yourself, bring attention back to your breath and body, again relaxing into the posture.

- Then bring to mind *someone who has been beneficial for you to know or know of,* someone who has inspired you or shown you great kindness. Recognizing that just as you wish to be happy and at peace, that benefactor likewise shares the universal desire for well-being and love, begin offering him or her these loving and kind phrases. Slowly repeat each phrase with that person in mind as the object of your well-wishing:

> "Just as I wish to be happy, peaceful, and free, may you too be happy."
>
> "May you be at ease."
>
> "May you be free from suffering."

Continue offering these phrases from your heart to your benefactor's, developing the feeling of kindness and response of love to others.

- When the mind gets lost in a story, memory, or fantasy, simply return to the practice. Begin again offering loving-kindness to the benefactor.

- After a few minutes of sending loving-kindness to the benefactor, let him or her go and return to your direct experience of the breath and body. Pay extra attention to your heart or emotional experience.

- Then bring to mind someone whom you do not know well, *someone who is neutral* (someone you neither love nor hate—perhaps someone you don't know at all, a person you saw during your day, walking down the street or waiting in line at the market). With the understanding that the desire for happiness and love is universal, begin offering that neutral person your loving-kindness phrases:

"May you be happy."

"May you be at ease."

"May you be free from suffering."

- After a few minutes of sending loving-kindness to the neutral person, bring attention back to your breath and body.

- Then expand the practice to include *family and friends toward whom your feelings may be mixed*—both loving and judgmental:

"May you be happy."

"May you be at ease."

"May you be free from suffering."

- After a few minutes of sending loving-kindness to the mixed category, bring attention back to your breath and body.

- Then expand the practice to include *the difficult people in your life and in the world*. (By *difficult* I mean those whom you have put out of your heart, those toward whom you hold resentment.) With even the most basic understanding of human nature, it will become clear that all beings wish to be met with love and kindness; all beings—even the annoying, unskillful, violent, confused, and unkind—wish to be happy. With this in mind and with the intention to free yourself from hatred, fear, and ill will, allow someone who is a source of difficulty in your mind or heart to be the object of your loving-kindness meditation. Meeting that person with the same phrases, pay close attention to your heart/mind's response:

"May you be happy."

"May you be at ease."

"May you be free from suffering."

- After a few minutes of practice in the direction of difficult people, begin to expand the field of loving-kindness to *all those who are in your immediate vicinity.* Start by sending phrases of loving-kindness to anyone in your home or building at the time of practice. Then gradually expand to those in your town or city, allowing your positive intention for meeting everyone with love and kindness to spread out in all directions. Imagine covering the whole world with these positive thoughts. Send loving-kindness to the north and south, east and west. Radiate an open heart and fearless mind to all beings in existence—those above and below, the seen and the unseen, those being born and those who are dying. With a boundless and friendly intention, begin to repeat the phrases:

"May all beings be happy."

"May all beings be at ease."

"May all beings be free from suffering."

- After a few minutes of sending loving-kindness to all beings everywhere, simply let go of the phrases and bring attention back to your breath and body, investigating the sensations and emotions that are present now.

- Then, whenever you are ready, allow your eyes to open and your attention to come back to your surroundings.

Chapter 9

KILL 'EM ALL (WITH KINDNESS)

situational response-ability based on the
compassionate act of killing the enemy

J ack Kornfield tells a story about a mother whose only child, a teenage boy, was killed in a gang war. The mother of the murdered child went to a court hearing of the young gang member who had killed her son and, with an icy and vengeful look in her eyes, told him, "I am going to kill you." The young gangster shrugged it off. He was on his way to prison for a very long time, and how was this old lady going to get to him anyway?

After the gang member had been in prison for some time, the mother of the boy he had killed began to visit him. Although he was suspicious of her motives, he accepted her visits, since no one from his family ever came to see him. She never mentioned her dead son; she spoke with what appeared to be friendliness, expressing concern for the prisoner's well-being and interest in his life. On a more concrete level, the mother put money in his commissary account and brought him books to read, or newspaper clippings about things she thought might interest him. They became so close that the boy began to think of this kind woman as the mother he'd never had. He felt great remorse for having killed her only child and thought that perhaps he was repaying his debt to her by allowing her to treat him as her child.

Years later, when the boy, who had grown into a man, came up for parole, the now elderly lady testified on his behalf, saying that she believed he had been rehabilitated. But she requested that, as a stipulation of his release, he be mandated into her custody, paroled to her home. The man, remembering her oath to kill him one day, began to wonder if this whole time she had just been plotting her revenge. But since he had nowhere else to go, and since he had truly grown to love this woman and for the most part trusted her, he agreed to being released into her custody. And so he was.

Sometime after having been released from prison, while eating dinner together one evening, the reformed gang member asked the old woman if she was still planning to kill him.

"I already have," she replied.

Her plan from the beginning had been to kill with kindness and forgiveness the murderer he had become. She told him that he was no longer that young boy who had killed her son; *that* person had died long ago, and he was now an honorable and trustworthy man. She said that he was free to leave her home anytime he pleased, but that she hoped he would stay. They cried together and then they laughed together, both enjoying the truth of her confession. And he stayed on with her, caring for her in her old age until she died some years later.

Our task as part of the 1%ers is to kill with kindness all of the causes of suffering. The Buddha first taught loving-kindness to a group of monks who had been practicing meditation in the forest. The monks had been experiencing great fear that the spirits of the forest did not want them there and would attack them. Probably they were just afraid of the dark! Their fear became anger toward the forest, and their anger became generalized ill will. And of course when someone feels angry, unsafe, and resentful, it becomes more and more difficult to meditate. So the monks went to the Buddha, asking for advice on how to deal with the perceived threat. The Buddha's advice was the teaching we just investigated, the Metta Sutta. He went into detail, offering the instructions we just read and urging the monks to wish for happiness and ease for all beings. It is said that after receiving these teachings on how to live a life of kindness with the desire and willingness not only not to cause harm but also to protect each other and all beings, the monks went back to the same place in the forest, but with a new attitude and outlook. As they recited the phrases of kindness, saying over and over, "May all beings be at ease," the forest began to feel safe; the fear of being attacked left them, and all of the beings of the forest began to appear friendly. Birds seemed to be singing sweet songs just for them; the mosquitoes seemed to leave them alone, and even when a mosquito or other bug did bite one of them, they were happy to be able to offer some sustenance to that life form. As their hearts became kind, their environment felt safe. Having killed the fear, they were free to practice meditation in peace.

Sometimes it is said that this experience of kindness is the antidote to fear, as well as to many other forms of suffering. It makes good sense that when we are coming from a place of kindness, we naturally experience the reflection of kindness from others.

My own life's experience has seemed to verify this teaching to a great extent. In my early life I was filled with anger, I was almost constantly dishonest, I caused great harm to many people, and I wished harm upon many others. I was living in an almost totally opposite way than is suggested in the Metta Sutta. I had no humility, no integrity, and no wish to protect anyone but myself. And living that way had me going in and out of jail regularly, addicted to drugs, and, most importantly, always looking over my shoulder to see if anyone was going to attack me. I felt completely, constantly unsafe. (Of course, crack cocaine has a way of making a person paranoid, but my fear was rooted in the chaotic reality of my life at that time.) Having stolen from so many people, I was always worried about getting caught. Living a life of drugs and crime, I was always afraid of the police. I was often in physical altercations, and the threat of violence on the streets was a real one. I knew nothing about being kind or loving; in fact, the world seemed to offer little more than violence and the suffering of living in fear. At the time I was so delusional that I often felt like I was the victim. That perspective was useful: it allowed me to justify the ways I was hurting other people by blaming my actions on the people who had hurt or betrayed me.

Of course, I now know that I had created the whole scene. In an unskillful reaction to the pain of my early years, I had created the life of crime, drugs, and violence that followed. Then—as I came to the practice of dharma and learned about the principles of metta—I slowly began to recreate that life by changing my ways of thinking and acting. It was not an overnight transformation by any means; a very gradual change took place—a change that's continuing even now, twenty-two years into the practice. But eventually, as I began to love myself and others, as I learned to be kind and eventually came to a sincere place of wanting all beings to be at ease, the world became a safer place for me. I used to get attacked, seemingly randomly, all of the time. It has now been over twenty years since anyone attacked me—not physically anyway. There has been some pretty hurtful gossip, but through long-term and intentional training of my heart through metta, I have often been successful at not taking harsh words too personally, and I have become quick to forgive. My life's experience has matched up with the Buddha's teaching that loving-kindness can make the world a safe place. It also feels a lot like the story I began with. That young drug addict that I was as a kid is dead. I killed him with metta.

All of that having been said, I have to acknowledge that this cannot always be true for everyone. I can't help but think of all the truly kind and loving people who were among those tortured and killed in Nazi concentration camps, in Communist Chinese "reeducation" prisons, in the cities and villages of civil-war-torn countries on the African continent, and in genocide of the native peoples of North America, to single out only a fraction of the violence in our world. I am also thinking of the millions of gays, lesbians, bisexuals, and transgendered folks that have been met with violence and hatred for no reason other than their natural sexual or gender orientation. I am sure that there have been hundreds of millions of truly kind people beaten and killed for one reason or another.

So how does a Buddhist reconcile him- or herself with all the violence and suffering in the world? Perhaps what the Buddha was pointing to in this teaching was more of an inner safety than a physical safety. I am thinking of the Tibetan Buddhist nun who is beaten and raped by Communist soldiers; her body is violated, the greatest trauma possible. But her years of kindness and compassionate practice allow her access to an internal place of safety, a source of loving-kindness that provides her with mercy and love and that meets her attackers with forgiveness and compassion. She understands the deep ignorance that these men are in, and she also understands the karmic hell they are creating for themselves. In such circumstances, metta does not protect us against being physically hurt, but it does have the potential to protect us from an immense amount of hatred and fear, and all of the suffering that comes with such emotions.

I believe that what I'm calling loving-kindness here—metta—does have the power to protect us from the extra layer of suf-

fering we create through greed, hatred, and delusion, and in
that way it does make the world (our inner world) a safer place.

The word *kindness* is often used as sort of a general term.
What is kind, colloquially speaking, depends on the circumstances. We could call it situational ethics. What is ethical
and kind in each situation will depend on varying factors. I'm
using the term *kindness* in a slightly different, specific way: to
be kind is to do whatever will end suffering in each situation.
The kind thing to do is the skillful response in each given
moment. For instance, when it comes to pleasurable experiences, the kind relationship to pleasure is almost always nonattached appreciation. If we can enjoy the pleasurable moments
without clinging to them or getting caught up in craving for
them to last forever, then we can avoid the typical suffering
we often create around pleasure. So the kind thing to do is
not get attached. But if we are not able to meet pleasure with
nonattached appreciation and consequently become attached to
pleasure, then the kind thing to do is let go. The next level
of kindness that's often called for is being patient with ourselves in the process of learning to let go. So then patience
becomes another act of kindness. And when our mind starts
judging us for not being very good at letting go and we respond with forgiveness, forgiveness is an act of kindness. Get
the picture? The kind thing to do depends on the situation,
yes—but it is always directed toward ending suffering. It does
not mean being fake nice all of the time; it means being real
and responsive to the suffering we experience ourselves and
perceive in others.

When it comes to painful experiences, the kind thing to do is almost always to meet the experience with compassion. Compassion ends suffering. As we saw earlier, it doesn't end *pain*, but it does take care of the extra level of suffering we tend to layer on top of our pain. In that way, then, the kindest thing we can do is cultivate tolerance and compassion toward pain.

One of the situations where kindness becomes tricky is when we are faced with the possibility that our seemingly kind actions could actually be causing some harm—in other words, that we could be enabling someone to suffer more through our intention to be kind. For instance, in the case of dealing with a friend or family member who is addicted to drugs, at some point in the relationship a strong boundary is going to have to be set. While lending money to a friend in many cases could be seen as a generous and kind act, with the addict it could actually be causing more harm than good. Most of us face this dilemma on some level or another on a regular basis—say, when asked for money on the street by someone who seems to be homeless and is obviously intoxicated. Is giving cash—something that may very well lead to further addiction and suffering—an act of kindness at all? In some cases the kindest thing we can do is say no. Sometimes kindness means telling individuals a truth they may not like hearing. At times kindness may even hurt the recipient while still remaining kind. I don't think kindness ever has the *intention* of causing harm, but in some situations harm is just unavoidable.

Some of the kindest things I've ever done for myself have been among the most difficult and painful experiences of my

life. For instance, when I started meditating, I found the retreats to be excruciatingly boring, and my body was in agony
much of the time, but I kept at it. Looking back, sticking with
meditation retreats was the kindest thing I have ever done for
myself and many, many others. What at the time truly sucked
eventually led to a radical change in my heart and mind. And
the positive changes in my life have allowed me to inspire and
encourage thousands of others to take the hard and transformative path of meditation retreats. The point is that kindness
comes in many different forms and from many different responses to different situations. We cannot say that generosity is
always kind or that causing pain is always unkind.

In the end our practice of kindness and situational ethics
becomes the way in which we kill the inner greed, hatred,
and fear. Not through violence but through love and kindness.
There is hope for external transformation only if the internal
revolution is firmly grounded in loving-kindness. We must
become the loving forces of a spiritual revolutionary front. It
may take only a handful of committed assassins to inspire a
full-fledged war against ignorance.

Part 3

AVOIDING THE DEAD END OF RELIGION

Chapter 10

GIVE IT UP

the power of generosity

I t is said that the first teaching that the Buddha gave to people he met on his travels through towns and villages was on the importance of generosity. It's a good first teaching for all of us. In the beginning of spiritual practice it is our goal to break through our internal greed and self-centeredness by external acts of giving. While generosity can originate from many different motivations and intentions, it almost always takes the form of giving. *What* we give can take many, many different forms, of course.

At times generosity takes the form of material giving. That type of giving is incredibly important. Whatever our income, we *all* have enough that we can give some to others. Our giving doesn't have to be done in big ways; indeed, it can and should be within our means. The Buddha often encouraged people simply to share some of their food with others who are in need. In the cities, towns, and villages of Southeast Asia, early each morning you can see people gathering outside their homes to offer food to the monastic communities as they pass by on their alms rounds. Those people who have more give more, and perhaps give more expensive foods. But even the poorest subsistence farmers give a handful of rice. The Thai people understand the importance of giving, and understand the Buddha's teaching that the merit accrued through giving depends not on the size of the gift, but only on the sincerity and heart-felt generosity of the giver. The Buddha said that if we knew the importance of generosity, we would never let a single meal go by without sharing it with someone who is in need. He was also clear that the goodness that comes from giving is always in accordance with the intention, sincerity, and means of the giver.

Intention is an important factor in generosity. In Buddhism, we understand that generosity not only allows us to overcome the suffering of clinging and selfishness, but it also generates good karma or merit. In the beginning of our practice of generosity, when we are still locked into the old ways of being self-ish, it is okay to give with the selfish intention of creating some good karma for ourselves. That is a low form of generosity, to be sure, but it is an understandable place to start. As wisdom develops, our intentions change. The actions may remain the same—still giving the handful of rice—but the intention begins to shift away from what we get from giving to just giving for the sake of giving and the joy of sharing our precious resources.

Merit is a real and important aspect of generosity, but it should not become or remain the soul intention behind our giving. I fear that in many Buddhist countries, the depth of the Buddhist path has been missed, having been replaced by a system of merit-making. I have spent much time in Southeast Asia, India, Sri Lanka, and Nepal, talking to native-born Buddhists about their relationship to Buddhism. There seems to be a common theme: that the priority of most Buddhists is not developing wisdom and compassion through meditative training; rather, it is following a boiled-down philosophy of making merit through giving to the monasteries, temples, and shrines. I guess this is why it is said that less than 10 percent of Buddhists actually meditate on a daily basis.

Making merit, while acknowledged by the Buddha, is not the most important aspect of the Buddha's dharma. It will not free us from suffering on its own. It is not enough to just be generous, especially if the gift-giving is motivated by what we will receive. As I said earlier, it is an okay place to start, but it is not a good place to remain. It is spiritual preschool, if you will. We all have to start somewhere, but hopefully we can make it into grade school, high school, and perhaps even college.

Giving does not have to be material or financial; in fact, it doesn't have to cost anything at all. We can give meaningfully and generously of our time and/or energy. Think about it: time is a precious resource—most of us feel like there aren't enough hours in the day to finish everything we want to do. So sharing some of our time with those who need it can be a true act of generosity and a great source of merit. Sitting beside a hospice patient is an incredible act of giving. Same for serving or preparing food at the local soup kitchen, visiting the elderly at a nursing home, or volunteering at the local homeless shelter or home for abused women, just to name a few. There are countless ways to give our time and energy to those who could use some help at a difficult time in their lives.

Another form of generosity consists of the giving of attention. I see this on two levels. One is the deep inner attention of meditative training, of paying close attention to ourselves. The other is the quality of being fully present and paying attention to the people we are with. In giving our full attention to people as an act of generosity, the meditative training allows us to be consistent and intentional. Without giving ourselves the gift of training our mind in concentration and mindfulness, we may find it incredibly difficult to be present for our friends, partners, and children. Our mind is all over the place, stuck in planning the day's activities, trying to remember something important that we meant to do, or lost in resentments, still rehashing a difficult conversation we had at work. So yes: meditation can be an act of generosity.

As mentioned in an earlier chapter, the Buddha referred to the untrained heart/mind as a monkey. The monkey doesn't have time to give its full attention to our kids, our lover, or anyone/anything else that is right in front of us. The monkey heart/mind is always chasing the banana. Taming the monkey, through meditation, is a great gift to oneself. It is perhaps the most generous thing we can do as we set off on the path to true happiness and freedom. And with the ability to pay attention—with the monkey finally at ease enough to sit still for a while—we can be fully present for others.

How much of what happens in therapists' offices is talking about how painful it was that our parents didn't pay enough attention to us, or that they didn't pay the right kind of attention? Or perhaps that they paid *too much* attention to us, engulfing us in their own monkey's obsession so that we became the banana! To be generous with our attention means also to be appropriate and discerning. There's nothing more annoying than meeting some pseudo-meditator type who gets right up in your face and stares into your eyes, clearly displaying how deeply attentive he or she is being. Come on, that's really not necessary. Relax.

We can be generous with anyone or anything, and we can and should include ourselves in the pool of recipients. Forgiveness is ultimately an act of generosity—as much to ourselves as to others. When we forgive others, the letting go of ill will and resentment is freeing for us as well as for the one forgiven—in fact, often more so. Because in the act of forgiveness we give ourselves a level of freedom we didn't have before, that act of generosity is not only an act of giving, but also an act of letting go. Generosity, like kindness, can be seen as the next wise thing to do. So it becomes generous to meditate. It becomes generous to be compassionate. It becomes generous to forgive.

All of the Buddha's dharma has the goal of ending suffering. As suffering decreases and eventually comes to an end, all that remains is a generous heart. When the Buddha had become enlightened, he didn't just hang around and cling to his freedom. Released from the suffering of attachment and aversion, he dedicated the rest of his life to serving the spiritual needs of the people. Generosity is the natural response of the enlightened heart. That generosity—the response of *each* liberated heart—can inspire millions and millions of people to be more kind, more generous, and more forgiving. The positive effect that our practice of the dharma has on the world makes each act of wisdom, compassion, and kindness an act of generosity. By changing ourselves, we are changing the world. When you understand this, it makes more and more sense to begin thinking along the lines of the bodhisattva ethic, which works "for the benefit of all living beings." I give "for the benefit of all living beings." I meditate "for the benefit of all living beings." I dedicate all of my life's energy "for the benefit of all living beings."

From this perspective, simply awakening, moving toward enlightenment, becomes an act of generosity. Meditation is one of the keys to unlocking the natural generosity of the heart. Underneath the greedy and selfish thoughts and feelings of the human condition lies a pure desire to help. We see this in our mindfulness practice: when we let go, there is a natural acceptance and feeling of care. But we cannot wait till there is no longer any attachment or fear to act. The act of giving is one of the ways to uncover the natural generosity that has been hidden by the fear and insecurity of greed. Each act of giving is a rebellion against selfishness. Each act of giving gets us closer to the true nature of the generous heart.

Chapter 11

THANX FOR THE GOOD TIMES

developing an attitude of gratitude

I am told that Chinese Buddhism has this saying: "Life is made up of ten thousand joys and ten thousand sorrows." We have already talked quite a bit about how to face the sorrows—through compassion, forgiveness, and kindness. But what about all the joys? How should we relate to all the pleasures in life?

The Buddha's second noble truth teaches us that much of our suffering is created by our craving for and attachment to pleasure. It is clear, then, that we do not want to get attached to pleasure. But we still want to experience it, don't we? Of course, the answer is a big fat juicy and pleasurable *yes*! Pleasure is not the problem. Pleasure is a natural and wonderful aspect of being alive. There are truly ten thousand joys to experience.

But what needs to be clearly understood is that pleasure is *always impermanent*: it *never* lasts long—it *never* has and it *never* will. Thus pleasure is not a reliable source of happiness. If you are still confusing pleasure with happiness, please stop. It's time to wake up. Time to see the truth about your life.

Pleasure is fleeting. Period. If we make pleasure the source of our happiness, we are happy only a fraction of the time. Worse yet, the rest of the time we're craving more pleasurable experiences, thereby missing what's happening right in front of us. We end up suffering through most of our lives, because there isn't ever enough pleasure, and when we *do* experience it, it doesn't last. Does this sound familiar? The Buddha was right about how we create suffering out of our craving for pleasure, wasn't he? We are not good at letting the ten thousand joys come, and letting them also go.

The other side of this equation is that when pleasure is happening—in those great moments of intimacy, beauty, adrenaline, and sensual pleasures—we all too often get so caught up in wanting the experience to last that we ruin the whole thing. This is the classic and daily experience of attachment. Attachment ruins pleasure. Clinging to the impermanent sunset, orgasm, bong hit, or even moment of mindfulness causes suffering. If we cling, we suffer. Attachment always hurts. Always!

The undeniable fact here on earth is that everything, including pleasure, is impermanent. When we cling to pleasure—as we do most of the time—we suffer. It's like trying to hold on to a rope that's being pulled out of our grasp: we don't have the strength to stop it; it's impossible. The outcome every time is rope burns, the suffering of clinging. Due to this truth, most of us, most of the time, are busy turning the ten thousand joys into ten thousand sorrows.

But perhaps surprisingly, the ten thousand joys and ten thousand sorrows stand in an ideal balance. For all of us in life, there will be pleasure and there will be pain, one counterbalancing the other. However, if we continue to attach our happiness to pleasure and remain in denial about the impermanent nature of all things, our life will fall out of balance and be more sorrowful than need be; we may have a life that's more like twenty thousand sorrows and very little joy.

The practice of mindfulness and the development of the metta principles of kindness, love, forgiveness, and humility will bring us closer and closer to creating a wise relationship to both pleasure and pain. As I have stated in previous chapters, *the only wise relationship to pain is mercy and compassion.* When it comes to pleasure, we find an equally simple equation: *the only wise relationship to pleasure is nonattached appreciation.* The more we learn to let go of clinging, the more we can enjoy pleasure. The less we are attached to or dependent on pleasure, the more we can be happy in the reality of each moment. True happiness is not dependent on life feeling good or being fun. True happiness comes through living in harmony with the ten thousand joys and ten thousand sorrows of life. This clearly means—and I have come to know this experience very well for myself— that we can be happy in the midst of sorrow or pain. Really, no bullshit here: when our heart learns to meet pain with compassion and pleasure with nonattached appreciation, then happiness can coexist with any sensation, emotion, or other experience. This is our goal, our intention, and our path. This is the happiness of the Buddha.

Another important aspect of appreciation that the Buddha taught is learning to enjoy the pleasures and successes of others without feeling threatened or jealous. The Buddha referred to this quality of the heart as appreciative or sympathetic joy. So much of our mental suffering is caused by the comparing and judging aspect of our mind—the part of us that feels jealousy. When someone else is happy or successful, we tend to feel angry or threatened due to our self-centeredness. Someone once said, "There's something not altogether displeasing about someone else's failure," and it's true; we often think, "Better him than me." Delighting in another's failure is the opposite of the feeling that the Buddha is talking about when he encourages us to be appreciative of other people's success, to have the physical experience of taking pleasure in the happiness of others. Underneath our feelings of envy and jealousy lies a pure appreciation of happiness in life—wherever it may be found, whoever's it is. Cultivating that appreciation, bringing it out from its hiddenness, is a difficult but necessary aspect of the dharma path. Appreciation balances compassion: we must acknowledge both the joys and the sorrows in life. If we get too focused on the sorrows, we will drown in the depths of suffering. The practice of appreciation allows us to acknowledge the joys that exist side by side with those sorrows.

Over my years of practicing appreciative joy meditations, I began to develop an ability to enjoy the pleasure and joy of others. It is a wonderful feeling to be able to cheer on others and feel happy for their successes and pleasures. More recently I have begun to see that this quality of appreciative joy does not pertain only to pleasure. As a dharma teacher and psychotherapist, I often have the pleasure of sitting with people who are having some very painful realizations about themselves. When these realizations are of the kind that I know will lead to a greater feeling of happiness and well-being in the future, I often experience this heart-quality of appreciative joy. In other words, sometimes I am happy when people are suffering, because I know that it is the *good* kind of suffering—the kind of suffering or pain that will ultimately lead to the end of suffering. Often when someone comes to me and spills his or her guts about how painful the meditative realizations have been, I smile and say how happy I am that this person is suffering so much. This might sound twisted, but it isn't. Waking up often involves a series of painful realizations, and to be happy that people are going through the hard work of awakening is a wholesome form of appreciation.

This heart-quality culminates in appreciating the preciousness of being alive. From the Buddhist perspective, where reincarnation is part of the fabric of reality, it is said that rebirth as a human is rare and precious. A famous Buddhist story compares our chances of being reborn human to the chances of a blind sea turtle (which surfaces only once every several thousand years) coming to the surface in the middle of a floating piece of hollowed-out wood—that is to say, there is only one piece of wood on the sea, and the turtle just happens to come to the surface in the center of it. You get the picture.

Human rebirth is precious, but it is not only being born human that is the trick. It is also being born into a realm where we have the chance to encounter the true dharma. It may be presumptuous for me to say so, but I will say it anyway: if you are reading this book, you are having such an incarnation. Whatever the circumstances of your life have been so far, it is clear that you have now encountered the dharma. The experience of hearing the truth about life is rare; thus you are having an incredibly rare incarnation. (I am in no way saying that I am the creator of this truth; I can take responsibility only for being a messenger. I am just representing the Rebel Saint, Siddhartha, "Sid," the Buddha.)

The point of our endeavor is to truly appreciate this life, to truly appreciate the dharma, to not waste any more time chasing delusions. Having taken birth as a human and additionally having come into contact with dharma is fortunate, but it isn't enough. Most people stop there. Or they get a taste of truth and vow to awaken and free themselves from delusion, only to shift into becoming one of the deluded Buddhist masses, mistaking buying merit or worshipping deities or teachers for the path. Please take these words to heart: if you appreciate the Buddha's teachings, don't get too lost in the religion of Buddhism. Just do what the Buddha encouraged.

There is so much goodness in every Buddhist tradition, but there is also so much that has nothing to do with the Buddha's message of liberation through personal effort. The more I understand about the Buddha and his teachings, the less I can accept the ways that some Buddhism is taught today. A lot of what is being taught by some schools of Buddhism is in direct contradiction to the Buddha's message. Some may say that I risk becoming a fundamentalist. Well yes, I would be happy—in this context—to stick with the fundamentals of liberation. Not out of superiority or competition, but out of concern for all the people who are sincerely seeking truth and are being misguided by so-called Buddhists as well as by the rest of the religious world.

Okay, let me step down off my soapbox for a minute. Where was I? Oh yeah, this incredible life we're living. And appreciating the opportunity we have to train our heart/mind to experience true happiness and real freedom from suffering. We don't know how long this life will last. Impermanence teaches us that nothing is certain or reliable, including these physical bodies of ours. The meditative reflections on death that are part of the Buddhist mindfulness practice and the preciousness of human rebirth are all in service of getting us motivated and grateful for the opportunity right in front of us—life.

Appreciative Joy Meditation

- Find a comfortable place to sit, and allow your attention to settle into the present-time experience of the body. Relax any physical tension that is being held in the body by softening the belly; relax the eyes and jaw and allow the shoulders to naturally fall away from the head.

- After a short period of settling into present-time awareness, begin to reflect on *your deepest desire for happiness or freedom from suffering.* Allow your heart's truest longing for truth and well-being to come into consciousness. With each breath, breathe into the heart's center the acknowledgment and appreciation of the joy and happiness you have experienced in your life.

- Slowly begin to *offer yourself appreciative and encouraging phrases* with the intention of uncovering the heart's sometimes hidden response of gratitude. Your phrases can be as simple as the following:

  > "May I learn to appreciate the happiness and joy I experience without clinging to it."

  > "May the joy I experience continue and grow."

  > "May I be filled with gratitude."

  If those phrases do not mean anything to you, create your own words to meditate on. Find a few simple phrases that have an appreciative intention, and slowly begin to offer these well-wishings to yourself.

- As you sit in meditation repeating these phrases in your mind, the attention will be drawn, as often happens in mindfulness meditation, back into thinking about other things or resisting and judging the practice or your own capacity for appreciation and gratitude. It takes a gentle and persistent effort to return to the next phrase each time the attention wanders:

"May I learn to appreciate the happiness and joy I experience without clinging to it."

Feel the breath and the body's response to each phrase.

"May the joy I experience grow."

Notice where the mind goes with each phrase.

"May I be filled with gratitude."

Allow the mind and body to relax into the reverberations of each phrase. Simply repeat these phrases over and over to yourself like a kind of mantra or statement of positive intention.

- Don't expect to feel grateful instantly through this practice. Sometimes all we see is our lack of appreciation and the judging mind's resistance. Simply acknowledge what is happening and continue to repeat the phrases, being as friendly and merciful with yourself as possible in the process.

- After a few minutes of sending these phrases of appreciation to yourself, bring the attention back to the breath and body, again relaxing into the posture.

- Then bring someone to mind *who has been beneficial for you to know or know of,* who has inspired you or brought joy to your life. Recognizing that just as you wish to be happy and successful in life, that benefactor likewise shares the universal desire to be met with encouragement, support, and appreciation, begin offering him or her the phrases.

- Slowly repeat each phrase with that person in mind as the object of your well-wishing:

    "Just as I wish to learn to appreciate the happiness and joy in life, may you too experience joy, and may you be filled with appreciation for your happiness and success."

    "May your happiness and joy increase."

    "May you be successful and be met with appreciation."

    Continue offering these phrases from your heart to your benefactor's, developing the feeling of appreciation in relationship to the joy and success of others.

- When the mind gets lost in a story, memory, or fantasy, simply return to the practice. Begin again offering appreciation and gratitude to the benefactor.

- After a few minutes of sending appreciation to the benefactor, let him or her go and return to your direct experience of the breath and body. Pay extra attention to your heart or emotional experience.

- Then bring to mind someone that you do not know well, *someone who is neutral.* Someone you neither love nor hate—perhaps someone you don't know at all, a person you saw during your day, walking down the street or waiting in line at the market. With the understanding that the desire for joy is universal, begin offering that person the appreciative phrases:

"May your happiness and joy increase."

"May the joy in your life continue and grow."

"May you be successful and be met with appreciation."

- After a few minutes of sending appreciation to the neutral person, bring attention to your breath and body.

- Then expand the practice to include *family and friends toward whom your feelings may be mixed*—both loving and judgmental:

"May your happiness and joy increase."

"May the joy in your life continue and grow."

"May you be successful and be met with appreciation."

- After a few minutes of sending appreciation to the mixed category, bring attention back to your breath and body.

- Then expand the practice to include the difficult people in your life and in the world. (By *difficult* I mean those whom you have put out of your heart, those toward whom you hold resentment.) With even the most basic understanding of human nature, it will become clear that all beings wish to be met with appreciation; all beings—even the annoying, unskillful, violent, confused, and unkind—wish to experience joy.

- With this in mind, and with the intention to free yourself from jealousy, fear, and ill will, allow *someone who is a source of difficulty in your mind or heart* to be the object of your appreciation meditation. Meet that person with the same phrases, paying close attention to your heart/mind's response:

  "May your happiness and joy increase."

  "May the joy in your life continue and grow."

  "May you be successful and be met with appreciation."

- After a few minutes of practice in the direction of difficult people, begin to expand the field of appreciation to *all those who are in your immediate vicinity.* Start by sending phrases of appreciation to anyone in your home or building at the time of practice. Then gradually expand to those in your town or city, allowing your positive intention for meeting everyone with appreciation to spread out in all directions. Imagine covering the whole world with these positive thoughts. Send appreciation to the west, then to the east, then to the north, then to the south. Radiate gratitude and appreciation to all beings in existence—those above and below, the seen and the unseen, those being born and those who are dying. With a boundless and friendly intention, begin to repeat the phrases of appreciative joy:

"May your happiness and joy increase."

"May the joy in your life continue and grow."

"May you be successful and be met with appreciation."

- After a few minutes of sending appreciation to all beings everywhere, simply let go of the phrases and bring attention back to your breath and body, investigating the sensations and emotions that are present now.

- Then, whenever you are ready, allow your eyes to open and your attention to come back to your surroundings.

Chapter 12

SURFING THE WAVES
OF KARMA

enjoying a mellow beach break or
bucking a fucking tsunami

One way of looking at the difficulties in our lives and in the world is through the lens of karma. If karma is a true law of the universe, then everything is unfolding based on causes and conditions. For some of you, this might be a radically new concept. Others of you might yawn and say, "Yeah, *karma*; I know all about that." I ask you to read this chapter with an open mind, but without blind faith. Consider the teachings here carefully and over a long period of time; please don't be too quick to decide that you know the answers.

What if everything that happens in this world is lawful and just? What if karma and reincarnation are completely true?

And what if all of the suffering in this world has truly been self-created? If everyone created the situation they find themselves in, does it mean we aren't responsible to help each other? Would you use karma as an excuse to harden your heart and rationalize your lack of compassion, or would you still have compassion for the suffering of others?

Let's look at an example. If we all got the parents we created, it was our own actions in our past lives that created our birth to, say, an alcoholic father and a codependent mother. Is compassion for our situation—and the situation of *all* children suffering in difficult and even dangerous families—still the appropriate response? What a different way of thinking about life that would be, if we were responsible for creating our family, rather than seeing ourselves as victims of our circumstances.

This is a difficult topic to tackle here. I fear that people will, as many millions have in the past, misunderstand karma and misuse it not only to absolve themselves of the responsibility to help each other, but also to rationalize why it's okay to oppress each other. I fear a reaction along the lines of "It's their karma, so it's okay if they're killed, or raped, or systematically oppressed because of their color, gender, religious beliefs, or sexual orientation." And this is not an unfounded fear. In fact, it's exactly what was happening in India at the time of the Buddha; it's precisely what he was addressing in teachings on equality and refuge for all who sought it. At that time, the religious power structure—Hinduism—was using karma to justify a racist form of oppression known as the "caste system," in which one's place in life was dictated by the circumstances of one's birth.

Despite the Buddha's work, this kind of ignorant misappropriation of karma continued throughout his life, and it continues to this day, even in societies not formally based on caste.

Using karma as justification for oppression is not much different than what some Christians did in the name of the Bible to rationalize slavery. Or what some fundamentalist Muslims do in the name of the Koran to justify the oppression of women. Or what some Japanese Buddhists did to justify, at various times and in various wars, the invasion of Korea, China, and the South Pacific and the bombing of Pearl Harbor. Western religions have used "God's will" as their justification for gross ignorance and violent behavior for the last two thousand years. Hindus have been using a twisted version of karma to justify the oppression of the above-mentioned caste system for more than three thousand years. Even Buddhists have done so!

The Buddha did his best to be clear that karma and reincarnation, intertwined as an integral part of his teaching, are in no way, on any level, a justifiable reason to oppress. Quite the opposite. If we are all creating our destiny and our destiny depends totally on how we act in each moment, then any time we cause any harm, we are causing ourselves harm. And karma includes not only our intentional actions, but also our intentional *inactions;* in other words, if we can help someone but we choose not to, we are karmically responsible for the selfishness that stopped us from getting involved. Any time you don't act in a compassionate way, saying, "It was their karma," that's just as great a sin or negative karmic action as if you had been the oppressor yourself. This is the real deal. The Germans who knew what was going on in Nazi Germany and could have helped but chose not to because they were afraid of what would happen to them are karmically implicit in the death of the Jews. The white people in this nation who don't act as allies to the people of color who continue to be systematically oppressed by law enforcement and a sociopolitical system designed to keep the masses segregated are karmically implicit in this ignorance and its consequences. The Brahman priest on the Ganges in India who won't touch or bless the "untouchable caste" will bear the fruit of his religiously justified racism. The Christian preacher who uses the Bible to justify his own homophobia and continues to mislead people about "homosexuality being a choice and a sin" will burn in a special kind of karmic hell created just for homophobes. You get the picture.

There are no karma-free zones in this world. No one is exempt from full responsibility for all his or her intentional actions and inactions. And no, ignorance is *not* an excuse. No, being misinformed by your religion is *not* an excuse. In our hearts we know that hurting any living being is wrong, no matter what our religion says. There are no loopholes. Everyone is fully responsible for what he or she does. Actions that cause harm have negative consequences, period—which may include an unfortunate rebirth. Actions that are wholesome and kind have positive outcomes, period—which may include a fortunate rebirth. If the law of karma is true, then this is a just and lawful world, all appearances to the contrary.

But whether we believe in karma and reincarnation or not, that perspective should not change our relationship to the suffering in this world. We are still responsible to try to help each other. We are still responsible for our actions. Whether the abused child was a real jerk in his last lifetime or not, our heart's response to suffering should always be a compassionate willingness to protect and forgive. Likewise in relation to the abuser or oppressor: even if she will eventually bear the consequences of her actions, that outcome should not be used as an excuse not to intervene. Ultimately, the trained heart would respond with equal compassion and understanding to both the abuser and the abused.

The Buddha addresses karma in his teaching on equanimity. Although the appropriate response to the suffering of the world is compassion, says the Buddha, that response has to be balanced with wisdom. Although we can care for and want to protect each other on a physical and even emotional level, ultimately we can't do anything to take away the internal attachment and identification with craving and aversion that creates suffering in others. In a desired state of equanimity—balance— we accept that fact: all beings have to do the work for themselves, everyone purifying his or her own karma; we can't do it for anyone else, and no one else can do it for us. This teaching must be understood on two levels. There is a level of physical suffering that we can and should do our best to alleviate. Then there is the more subtle level of internal suffering, due to clinging and aversion, that we have no control over in others. This second level is what equanimity points toward.

Equanimity highlights the fact that only the individual has the ability to transform his or her relationship to the heart/

mind. We cannot force people to be free; everyone has to do the work him- or herself. Practice in this realm of equanimity involves opening up to the understanding of the balance of compassion with humility. Although we may have the greatest intentions to free all beings from suffering—and there is a lot we *can* do through practicing generosity and kindness—equanimity shows us that ultimately all beings have to free themselves. Don't get too attached to world peace, or even to your partner's happiness. What we can and should be doing is trying to educate, support, and encourage each other to develop more wisdom and compassion.

Equanimity Meditation Instructions

- Find a comfortable place to sit, and allow your attention to settle into the present-time experience of the body. Relax any physical tension that is being held in the body by softening the belly; relax the eyes and jaw and allow your shoulders to naturally fall away from the head.

- After a short period of settling into present-time awareness, begin to reflect on your deepest desire for happiness and freedom from suffering for both yourself and others. Reflect on your desire to serve the needs of others and to be compassionately engaged in the world. Reflect on both the joy and the sorrow that exist in the world. Allow your heart's truest longing for truth and well-being to come into consciousness.

- With each breath, breathe into the heart's center the acknowledgment of the need to balance your pure intention of creating positive change with the reality of your inability to control others.

- Begin repeating the following phrases:

  "All beings are responsible for their own actions."

  "Suffering or happiness is created through one's relationship to experience, not by experience itself."

  "The freedom and happiness of others is dependent on their actions, not on my wishes for them."

  Relax into the reverberations of this balance between harmonizing the heart's deepest desire to help others with the mind's wise response of acknowledging our limitations and powerlessness.

- Continue to repeat these phrases for as long as feels appropriate. Perhaps ten to twenty minutes is a good amount of time to start with.

Chapter 13

TONGLEN: A NEW-SCHOOL TWIST ON AN OLD-SCHOOL PRACTICE

breathing it all in, breathing it all out

Among the original teachings of the Buddha are practices called the Brahma Viharas (or "sublime states"). In these teachings, he gave meditation instructions in the primary heart-training practices of loving-kindness, compassion, appreciation, and equanimity. These practices were so popular that later Buddhists developed many more techniques, all aiming at the same goal of uncovering compassion and love for all beings. Although I tend to be a bit of an old-school elitist (of the Theravada tradition), I am also happy to incorporate beneficial teachings and techniques that came along later (with the Mahayana tradition).

In my view, whatever works, works. Metta is the old school. Tonglen is the new school. I consider myself an American Buddhist. I incorporate the teachings that make the most sense from all of the Asian traditions.

Tonglen is a Tibetan word that means "sending and taking" or "giving and receiving." The foundation of the practice is to breathe in pain and suffering and to breathe out compassion. In metta practice we simply train the mind by wishing for all beings to be at ease; it is assumed that we are already aware of the great pain and suffering in the world, and our wishes are in response to that suffering. In the practice of tonglen, it is not assumed that we are fully aware of the suffering in the world; we are asked to think about the pain in our lives, in the lives of others, and in the world, and indeed to breathe in that pain and suffering directly. This is the "taking in" or "receiving" aspect of the practice. On the in-breath you are willing to feel the pain, to acknowledge the great amount of suffering in your life and in the world. This is an act of bravery in that it requires a willingness to drop all forms of denial, to see the world as it is.

The in-breath of tonglen is the practice of Buddhism's first noble truth. In that truth the Buddha asks us to "fully know the truth of suffering." Sometimes we are half-assed about the acknowledgment of suffering. Tonglen allows us to take that suffering in fully. Sometimes people are afraid of turning toward suffering; they feel that it will overwhelm them. But all we are doing in tonglen is looking, consciously and directly, at what has always been there. Just because we don't look at the elephant in the room doesn't mean it hasn't been there the whole time. And when we *do* begin to look at the truth of the situation that we and the world are in, it's liberating rather than overwhelming. It can be a great relief to turn toward the truth of suffering, because it allows us to finally make sense of why life is so often difficult, why people are so often unkind: because everyone is suffering on some level. So we breathe in the truth. It may hurt a little at first, but that's the point: it *should* hurt. There's nothing wrong with feeling some pain. Pain is not the enemy. Pain is not the cause of suffering. Pain is part of life. Pain is a problem only when we meet it with hatred or ignore it. But in tonglen we are not ignoring it; we are breathing it in, feeling it, and responding to it.

After breathing in the pain, we breathe out compassion. As we already know, the only wise relationship to pain is compassion. But it is often difficult to find the ability to respond with mercy, compassion, or forgiveness. Tonglen gives us a practical way to train our heart/mind to access compassion through the repetition of intentionally trying to meet the pain we've inhaled with a compassionate exhale. Of course, it's not as simple as "just breathing out compassion," because in the beginning we don't have the ability to do so in a genuine and sincere way. But as with everything, the disciplined and repetitive action of meditation allows us access to unknown heart-qualities.

Tonglen does not *create* compassion; it simply allows us access to the compassionate heart that has been buried beneath the aversive tendencies of the untrained heart. With each out-breath that intends to meet the pain with compassion, we get closer and closer to the true heart's loving response of compassion. Breathing out compassion is letting go of needing the pain to go away. It is letting go of any extra layers of resistance, judgment, or fear that we have piled on top of the pain. Compassion doesn't end pain, as we've seen—but it does end suffering about pain. So as we breathe out, we don't have the expectation that our compassionate intention is going to magically make the pain disappear, but we do hold to the understanding that compassion can and will change how we relate to pain.

In striving to understand tonglen and other dharma practices, I think about a simile that my father used to use when teaching forgiveness or compassion. He would say that each one of our unskillful reactions to life—usually some form of clinging or aversion—is like a thin sheet of rice paper that we lay over our heart. Think about how many sheets of fear, of anger, of resentment, of judgment we lay over our heart each day! We do it constantly, until eventually our heart is buried beneath such a thick wall of paper that it becomes bulletproof. Each piece of paper in itself is not a problem; it's just rice paper—it dissolves in water, or we can break through it with the flick of a finger. But when our habitual reactive tendencies of clinging and aversion go unchecked, the paper becomes thicker and thicker until it becomes like armor.

All of the Brahma Vihara practices and tonglen have the ability to initiate the process of dissolving the armoring of the heart. Each time we repeat our metta phrases or breathe out compassion in tonglen, we are dissolving the rice paper; we're getting closer and closer to our true heart's natural compassion. For some of us it may take a while to be able to truly feel the compassion we are trying to access with tonglen, but I ask you to have faith that eventually you will uncover and recover your heart.

Tonglen Meditation Instructions

- Find a comfortable posture—one that is alert and upright, but relaxed and soft. Allow your eyes to close and bring full attention into your heart's center. Allow the breath to feel as though it were entering and exiting directly through the heart.

- Now simply *breathe in the generalized suffering in the world* that you are aware of. Allow your heart to open and be filled with the sorrow of the world. Feel that pain, that grief, that sorrow. Let it all in.

- Then breathe it all out, *exhaling waves of compassion in all directions.* Send mercy and forgiveness to all living beings, to the whole world.

- Do this over and over—breathing in the suffering, breathing out compassion.

- After a few minutes of that generalized giving and receiving, begin to add a visual quality to your meditation.

- As you breathe in, *visualize the pain and suffering* as black, heavy, and hot. Breathe in the dark fire of the world's sorrow.

- As you exhale, *visualize the mercy and compassion* as white, light, and cool. Breathe out the soothing, cool ice of compassion.

- Continue the hot/cold breathing for a few minutes.

- Next we come to the personal aspect of the practice. Bringing to mind *specific situations in your life that are painful,* breathe into your heart the pain of your life situation, feeling it completely. Breathe out mercy and compassion for yourself. Over and over, breathe in suffering and breathe out compassion.

- After a few minutes of the practice with your personal difficulties, begin to expand again. This time include *people in your life whom you love.* Breathe in the pain and sorrow of your loved ones. See it as heavy, dark, and hot. Breathe out compassion for their suffering, experiencing the out-breath as light, white, and cooling. Breathe in the sorrow; breathe out loving, caring, and compassion.

- After a few minutes with loved ones, expand to include *all of the people whom you do not already love.* Include the pain and sorrow of the masses and even of your enemies. Everyone is suffering on one level or another, just as you are. Breathe in the suffering of humanity;

breathe out compassion for humanity. Breathe in the pain that closes the heart of your enemies; breathe out the compassion that heals the wounds which have created the unskillful actions of your enemies.

- Work with this level for as long as it takes to begin to mean it. Eventually you will sincerely care for the suffering of all living beings, including the most unskillful of your enemies.

- Finally, let go of the personal levels of your life and of the human realm and expand the practice in all directions to include *all forms of life*. Include animals, insects, birds, fish, and so on. Breathe in the pain and suffering of all living beings; breathe out compassion and love for all the world. Experience your in-breath as black, heavy, and hot; your out-breath as white, light, and cool. *Remember to include yourself* in this last section. You are part of the interconnected web of existence.

- After some time, let go of the visualization and just breathe normally. Feel your breath and body. Pay attention to your heart and mind.

- End the practice with a simple statement such as, "May I awaken the compassionate heart, for the benefit of all living beings."

Chapter 14

IS THIS HEAVEN OR
IS THIS HELL?

choosing to get free or to wander
through the realms forever

In Buddhist cosmology it is taught that there are six differ-ent realms into which we can be born. Only two of the six—the human and animal realms—are visible to the human eye. The full list of realms is as follows:

1. Heavenly realm (within which there are twenty-seven levels)

2. Jealous gods

3. Humans

4. Animals

5. Hungry ghosts

6. Hell realm (with only a few levels)

These realms are often portrayed in Buddhist art via the Wheel of Life, a large circle held by Yama, the deity that personifies death. In the center of the wheel is a smaller circle, or hub, containing artistic renditions of greed, hatred, and delusion, often represented by animal totems—the rooster is greed, the snake is hatred, and the pig is delusion. It is greed, hatred, and delusion that keep the wheel spinning and keep the individual wandering from realm to realm. The large part of the circle is cut, pielike, into six slices or sections, with each section representing one of the realms of existence. Outside of the wheel is the Buddha, and Nirvana. Interestingly, though, the Buddha also shows up in each realm as an example of freedom within a level of suffering.

The heavenly realm is usually depicted as a place of pleasure and abundance, where all beings are enjoying themselves—satisfied and happy. The only problem in heaven seems to be that it's so pleasant there that there's no motivation to end attachment. An illusion is created when you are able to satisfy every desire, but even heaven is impermanent; it can't last forever. (*All* of the realms are impermanent, because they fall within *samsara*—the Buddhist "sea of existence" referred to in an earlier chapter, encompassing both the world we know and the world that we cannot see—which by definition is impermanent.) For most of the citizens of the heavenly realm, still shedding vestiges of attachment, there is more work to be done. For some it is just a place to burn off the last bit of karma before Nirvana.

The realm of the jealous gods is also a realm of abundance, but the inhabitants are not happy with what they have. They are suffering from terrible jealousy, because there is a tree that has its roots in their realm but its ripening fruits in the heavenly realm directly above them. The jealous gods have thus waged war against the heavenly realm. They live in a state of wanting what they do not have.

The human realm is part of the world we know—the world of joy and sorrow, pleasure and pain, gain and loss. The human realm is depicted as having great ignorance and suffering as well as great wisdom and ability to transform through meditative training.

The animal realm is also part of the world we know. We can see most of the animal realm; it includes mammals, fish, birds, insects, and other species. This realm is considered a state of instinctual survival; it is characterized by an almost constant threat of being killed by a larger predator. With fear, lust, and violence ruling the animal realm, there is not much role for free will.

The realm of the hungry ghosts is unseen to the human eye. Like the realm of the jealous gods, it is a realm of abundance. Every food a creature could want is there, but the realm is inhabited by large-bodied, monster-like creatures that have such a teeny-tiny, pinhole-size mouth that they can't get any of the delicious foods into their bodies. The hungry ghosts live in a state of constant craving and constant dissatisfaction—a state very similar to addiction.

The multilevel hell realm is a place of intense pain and suffering. Demons torture this realm's denizens with fire, ice, and fingernails on the chalkboard. The pain in hell is constant and unavoidable—so overwhelming that it is nearly impossible to meet it with compassion. The good news is that hell is impermanent too.

Although it could very well be true that these six realms are actual physical realms into which people are reborn, I find it just as likely that this teaching is merely an analogy for our varied human experience. These realms are states of the heart/mind as well as states of being. To illustrate, let's look at this from the perspective of the heart. From this perspective, hell would be a broken heart, and heaven would be the honeymoon period of falling in love. Let's see if we can extend this analogy further.

As I said earlier, an image of the Buddha appears in each of these realms, representing the enlightened potential of our heart, or what some schools of Buddhism call our "Buddha nature." In the hell realm, the Buddha is our heart's potential to have compassion and forgiveness. Even in the midst of the greatest heartbreak, grief, or life-threatening illness or injury, we still have the potential to meet our pain with mercy, compassion, and forgiveness. The Buddha shows up in hell to be an example of the capacity of the heart to enter the hellish experiences of life. When our heart is open, purified, and radiating kindness, compassion, mercy, and forgiveness, life will still at times become painful enough to feel like hell. An enlightened heart doesn't spare us that; it just gives us the capacity to meet all that life offers with love.

In the realm and experience of the hungry ghosts, the Buddha is our heart's ability to meet our constant and insatiable cravings with mercy and acceptance. At times we can even become generous to the other starving beings in the midst of our own suffering. The heart of metta is called to respond to the suffering of craving. The heart's generosity can overcome our cravings. The heart's equanimity can meet the suffering of craving and addiction without becoming codependent or enabling.

In the animal realm, the Buddha is the heart's ability to practice renunciation even in the midst of animal-like survival instincts, to be kind even when we are afraid and insecure. The heart is called upon to be willing to tolerate danger, real or imagined, in the animal realm—to be willing to sit in the fire of lust or anger without acting unskillfully. Without the heart's wisdom, when we are in an animal-like state of mind we habitually react to fear and anger with violence and to lust with indulgence. With meditative training our heart allows us to evolve out of being ruled by the animal instincts, and we can finally become human. But as we now understand, being human isn't all that evolved either.

The Buddha appears in the human realm as an example of the heart's potential for equanimity, the perfect balance of wisdom and compassion in a realm that has the perfect balance of pleasure and pain. Halfway between heaven and hell, humans are ideally suited for enlightenment. But the cravings and aversions that are built into the human heart/mind and body have great potential to hinder the individuals' willingness to take on and follow through with the long-term task of training the heart to respond with wisdom and compassion. The Buddha represents the truth of our heart's potential to fully awaken in this lifetime.

The Buddha's presence in the realm of the jealous gods bears witness to the heart's ability to accept what is offered, to enjoy what is present with appreciation and gratitude. It is our heart's potential for appreciation and gratitude for what is. When our heart is open and wise, we are free from jealousy. When we have uncovered and developed the appreciative heart, we are content and at ease. The Buddha aspect of us is happy for the gods above, who enjoy the fruits of our labor.

In the heavenly realm, the Buddha is our heart's ability to enjoy impermanent pleasures without clinging to them. The Buddha understands impermanence, yet indulges with appreciative nonclinging to the heavenly realm. We have to guard against the tendency to think that suffering is noble and heavenly enjoyment is overindulgent. With a wise heart, a heart filled with metta for all living beings, it is an act of generosity to allow ourselves to bask in the sun on the beach for the day. To enjoy a delicious and perhaps expensive meal or to spend the day in bed with our lover, getting up only occasionally to get some more ice cream. Heavenly realms come and go. We don't have to avoid them—indeed, we should *enjoy* them—but we must not cling to them or spend all of our time trying to create them.

In this life we are constantly wandering through these six realms. We claim to be human, but how often are we actually behaving like animals, ghosts, or jealous gods? With an untrained heart we are destined to wander endlessly from realm to realm—this is the definition of *samsara*. As long as greed, hatred, and delusion remain in control of our heart, our destiny will continue to inhabit hell and the ghost realms, with the occasional stopover in momentary heavens.

The path to end suffering, to liberate the heart, is clearly laid out for us. If we can bring mindfulness to our moment-to-moment experience, metta will become our guide to liberation from this cycle of suffering. Uncovering our heart's deepest and most innate wisdom will free us from the wheel of perpetual wandering. Then, if we are so inclined, we will have the ability to intentionally and volitionally visit the six realms—but, as with the Buddha, as an example of freedom.

Chapter 15

WHAT'S YOUR SIGN?

diagnosing your personality type
(but not letting it define you)

From a Buddhist perspective, we all have a personality type—one of three kinds. How that personality type comes about—whether it's karmic (based on past lives) or conditioned (based on experiences we have in this life)—is debatable. For the sake of this chapter I will stay out of the origination-of-personality debate. Here I will simply investigate the truth of our personality tendencies and how we can diagnose ourselves and others, and ultimately how we can use the information we have about ourselves and others to create more harmony and less suffering in our lives.

Traditionally, Buddhism classifies personalities into three categories, each one based on one of the three root causes of suffering: greed, hatred, and delusion. Most likely we all have a bit of all three tendencies—moments of greed, moments of hatred, and periods of delusion. Although it is true that all un-enlightened beings do suffer all three of these experiences, it is thought that each of us has a core operating tendency toward one or another. Some people react with desire to most situations, some with aversion, and some without noticing what's going on. You may have noticed that Buddhism diagnoses the personality based on the negative traits, but we don't stop there. There's also a positive side to each of these personality types: confidence, discernment, and serenity:

- Greedy/craving/confident type

- Hating/aversive/discerning type

- Deluded/spaced-out/serene type

Early on in my studies of Buddhism, I was taught the following classic exercise for use in diagnosing oneself (and perhaps others): Upon first entering a room, do you first notice what you like about the room, or what you don't like about the room? Alternatively, do you not notice much about the room at all because you're preoccupied with yourself? How you answer reveals your personality type.

People with the greedy/craving/confident personality type will first notice what they like and perhaps want in the room. For instance, "I really like that piece of art; where can I get something like that?" Or "That's a great couch; I wonder how much it cost. Could I afford a couch like that?" The greedy type has a tendency toward wanting and also has confidence in obtaining the desired objects or objectives. Of course, after a bout of craving, such personalities may also notice what they *don't* like: "That's a great couch, but that carpet is hideous!" Or "That painting is beautiful! Too bad they don't have it lit correctly."

On the other hand, people of the hating/aversive/discerning type would first notice what they *don't* like about the room. For instance, "That's the ugliest carpet I've ever seen!" Or "This place is dark and musty. Can someone please open a window?" Hatred-based types pick out what they don't like about the situation first. But because their strength is discernment in making judgments, they may also come around to seeing the things that they *do* like. "On the other hand, this is a very comfortable couch. And that ill-lit painting is amazing. I wonder who painted it?"

Finally, people of the deluded/spaced-out/serene type don't notice the art, the couch, or anything else about the room right away. They are too lost in their own world. "I wonder how these pants look on my ass?" Or "I hope that there are some cute girls at this party." Or "I wonder why the earth rotates clockwise around the sun rather than counterclockwise?" The deluded types are already sitting on the brown-leather, goose-down-stuffed couch staring at the ugly carpet, completely oblivious to their surroundings. Of course, they are also not suffering as much about their cravings or aversions as their other-type peers; in fact, they probably appear perfectly serene in their delusional world of self-centeredness. Eventually they too may lust after the painting or the couch, but it probably won't be their initial response to the room.

Let's run through the three types again, in more detail.

In conversation and relationship, people of the greed-based type may come across as positive, often agreeable, and perhaps extroverted. Confidence and faith are the positive flip sides of greed and craving. These folks want a lot, and they have faith that they can get it. When it comes to a *meditative* greed-based type, these searchers may suffer from a craving for spiritual experiences, and from a lack of patience and a lot of lustful thoughts during meditation practice. But they will often also have discipline and confidence in the Buddhist path. They want enlightenment and are willing to work hard for it—that is, if they don't get misled into some feel-good, New Age promise of bliss from chanting, or "ten easy steps to quick and cheap liberation." Greedy-type people have probably tried a lot of so-called spiritual paths before arriving at the Buddhist discipline. Given their greed—their desire to have fulfillment *now*—they need to be alert for false teachers and dharma scams. They can get into all kinds of trouble if their desire isn't balanced with discernment.

People of the hatred type often come off as negative. It can be difficult to be in relationship and unpleasant to be in conversation with people who like to point out your flaws. The hatred type, if really imbalanced, can sink into deep depressions and suicidal tendencies: it's hard to function when you're constantly seeing the negative side of things, when everything could always be better than it is. Life is filled with too much pain and too many stupid people for the aversive type. The positive flip side is that some of what the hatred types think and feel may be true. There is often discernment and fierce wisdom mixed in with the judgment and negativity. A meditating aversive type could progress quickly and see with wisdom and discernment the causes of suffering. Such folks may have difficulty in relating to teachers and may also suffer from rejecting community. Overall, though, hatred-based types can make for great meditators if they can channel their aversion toward the true causes of suffering and vow to end it all, *including the hatred itself.*

Delusional types may be easy to get along with and also have an easy time of meditation initially. They typically find a sense of peace and serenity easy to cultivate, but they have to be very disciplined in the effort of staying present and not floating off into la-la land. For delusional types, mindfulness and concentration are key to a successful meditation practice. The precision that comes from intentional present-time awareness will balance and refine the deluded mind-state.

All of these personality types need to be met with the appropriate heart-response. People of the greedy type will need to put great effort into becoming generous and nonattached to getting more. Those of the hatred-based type will need to focus intensely on forgiveness and compassion. The delusional types will need, through mindfulness, to come into contact with their greed and hatred so that they can offer the antidotes of forgiveness and generosity as their wise heart-response.

I encourage you to diagnose yourself, if you haven't already. I believe that such diagnosis can be a skillful tool in the process of awakening the heart. I have also found it incredibly liberating to get a sense of the personality types of others. Discovering that our partners, friends, or co-workers don't have the same initial experience of things as we do can help us develop compassion, be forgiving, and be accepting.

Remember, though, that these personality types are not *all* of who we are. Be careful not to get too identified with your personality tendencies. Rather, hold all of this lightly and with a playful attitude.

Conclusion

HEARTFULNESS— LIVING A LIFE BASED ON KIND AWARENESS

I t is my hope that you will take the teachings and practices in this book and digest them fully in your own way and in your own time, applying what makes sense to *you*. These teachings are not simply theory to be believed or understood; they are practical tools to be developed and integrated into one's daily life. The dharma described in these pages is a path, a practice, and a new way of relating to ourselves and others. Some say that Buddhism offers a liberation that has two wings, the wing of compassion and the wing of wisdom; others speak of the distinction between heart and mind. My current feeling is that these are false dualities. There is only one thing that needs to be done, and that is to live a life of heartfulness. Heartfulness encompasses everything. Mindfulness is heartfulness; forgiveness is heartfulness; compassion is heartfulness;

appreciation is heartfulness; even understanding impermanence and the truth of suffering is heartfulness.

Our practice and goal is to live a life that is full of the positive and wise qualities of heart. The untrained heart is not yet trustworthy, while the trained heart is fully and completely a safe refuge. With the long-term and consistent application of the meditations offered here, your heart will become free from the obscurations of greed, hatred, and delusion. You will perfect your relationship to being; your perspective will become heartful and therefore trustworthy.

You don't have to run off to a monastery to walk this path, although for some that is a noble and wise calling. I am primarily interested in dharma as a practical and applicable way of life in the everyday world of working and relationships. I think that our American form of Buddhism, as it grows and evolves, is going to be primarily a path of householders, rather than of monks or nuns.

What is important, though—wherever we find ourselves on this path—is the support of others. We need teachers and communities that inspire and support us on the path of heartfulness, because the journey is fraught with many dangers and a lot of personal responsibility. There are many great teachers out there, and many great and trustworthy communities. But there may be an equal number of teachers and communities that are not so trustworthy. As a student of the path, you will have to use your own discernment about these things. Just because some particular teacher calls it Buddhism doesn't mean that what's taught has much to do with what the Buddha himself actually taught. As a student of Buddhism, the responsibility lies on *you* to study, learn, and discern the dharma for yourself. You must also be careful with how you relate to teachers. The Buddha was clear and insistent on the point of personal responsibility and liberation through one's own effort. Teachers are here only to point out the path; you must do all of the trudging yourself. Make sure that your teachers are walking a heartful path and teaching a heartful approach to real life.

As I began this book with a warning, I will also end with one. The true Buddhist path is rare and difficult. Along the way you will be asked to face the most difficult of human emotions and challenges. The great news is that you have the capacity to awaken in this lifetime! All you need is the perseverance to train your heart/mind thoroughly. Along the way you will meet many other spiritual revolutionaries. Some will become lifelong friends on the path; many will fall by the wayside, drawn back into the matrix of greed and hatred. Those of us who commit and stay the course are the 1%ers of dharma, the forgiving few, the dharma ninja assassins, the real revolutionaries who can change the world. I hope to meet you along the way. May our paths cross soon on this journey of the heart.

Noah Levine

DHARMA LISTS YOU MIGHT FIND USEFUL

Four Noble Truths

1. *Dukkha.* There is a lot of suffering in life. Some of it is self-created; some is unavoidable.

2. *Tanha.* The cause of most of the self-created suffering in life is craving, attachment, and aversion.

3. *Nibbana.* The end of suffering is attainable in this lifetime. It will come as a result of the extinguishing of the flames of greed, hatred, and delusion.

4. *The Eightfold Path.* The path to end suffering consists of the following eight training factors:

   Understanding reality as it is

   Intentionally living in a wise and compassionate way

Speaking what is true and useful

Acting with nonviolent, honest, and sober integrity

Working in a wise and nonharming profession

Energetically training the heart/mind

Mindfully bringing awareness to each moment

Concentrating attention on the impermanent unfolding of the present

Brahma Viharas

1. *Metta.* A detailed and deliberate training of our hearts to be filled with *loving-kindness,* forgiveness, and humility.

2. *Karuna.* The ability to respond to pain with *compassion.*

3. *Mudita.* The ability to respond to pleasure with *appreciation.*

4. *Uppekha.* The balancing heart-quality of *nonattachment.*

Four Foundations of Mindfulness

1. *Body Awareness.* Awareness of such physical components as the breath, posture, activities (including eating and walking meditation), the four elements, the thirty-two parts of the body, and reflections on death.

2. *Feeling Tone.* Awareness of the pleasant, unpleasant, or neutral feeling tone of each object of awareness.

3. *Mind Objects.* Awareness of both the processes and contents of the mind.

4. *Truths.* Moment-to-moment nonjudgmental awareness of what is true. This includes mindfulness of the four noble truths, the five hindrances, the seven factors of enlightenment, etc.

Five Hindrances

1. Craving for pleasure

2. Aversion to pain

3. Restlessness

4. Sloth

5. Doubt

Seven Factors of Enlightenment

1. Mindfulness

2. Investigation

3. Effort

4. Joy

5. Tranquility

6. Concentration

7. Equanimity

Twelve Links of Dependent Arising

This linked listing is the Buddha's description of how we perpetuate unhappiness. As the description reveals, everything is connected. Kind awareness is the key to breaking the cycle of suffering. By bringing attention to the eighth and ninth links of dependent arising, we can begin to choose to respond with kind acts of compassion to pain and with nonclinging to pleasure.

1. Ignorance, which leads to

2. Mental formations (thoughts or emotions), which lead to

3. Consciousness, which requires

4. Name and form, which has

5. Six senses (physical sensation, hearing, seeing, smelling, tasting, and mental thoughts) through which stimuli generate

6. Contact, which creates sense impressions that generate

7. Feelings (pleasant, unpleasant, or neutral) that generate

8. Craving (either to keep or to get rid of the feeling), which causes

9. Grasping (or aversion), which generates

10. Becoming (identifying with the experience as personal), which generates

11. Birth (incarnating around the grasping), which generates

12. Suffering or dissatisfaction

Five Fetters (or Piles)

1. The body

2. The sense impressions or feeling tones of the body

3. The mind and the objects of the thinking mind (including thoughts and the roots of emotions)

4. Perception (including memory)

5. Consciousness

Three Personality Types

1. Greedy/craving/confident

2. Hating/aversive/discerning

3. Deluded/spaced-out/serene

Three Poisons/Flames/Fuel for Samsara

1. Greed—attachment and craving

2. Hatred—aversion and anger

3. Delusion—self-centeredness and belief in permanence

Three Elements of Forgiveness

1. Asking for forgiveness from those whom we have harmed

2. Offering forgiveness to those by whom we have been harmed

3. Forgiving ourselves for everything

THANX

As with everything in existence, this book arose out of causes and conditions. I would like to acknowledge and express gratitude to some of the people who helped this book come into fruition. All of my teachers, especially Jack Kornfield and Ajahn Amaro, Stephen and Ondrea Levine, Howie Cohn, Joseph Goldstein, Sharon Salzberg, and Stephen and Martine Batchelor. My agent, Loretta Barrett. My editors, Eric Brandt and Cynthia DiTiberio. My colleagues, the 1% posse, Vinny Ferraro, JoAnna Harper, Pablo Das, Kyira Korrigan, Jason Murphy, Mary Stancavage, Matthew Brensilver, Ron Ames, Stephanie Tate, Scott Spencer, Doug Achert, Josh Korda, Jake Cahil, Joseph Rogers, Enrique Calazo, Jordan Kramer, Silke Tudor, and the rest of the teachers and facilitators from Against The Stream worldwide. Much Respect to all the groups and members around the world in the Against the Stream and Dharma Punx communities; DIY in Vancouver, NYC Dharma Punx, Urban Dharma SF, Boston DP, Austin DP, Seattle DP, Rebel Dharma SC, Portland

DP, Houston DP, Berkshire DP, Hudson Valley DP, Philly DP, Jersey DP, Baltimore DP, Baton Rouge DP, Dallas DP, San Diego DP and ATS SD, New Haven, Front Range–Denver, Boulder, Fort Collins DP, Phoenix DP, ATS Belgium and Holland, ATS/ DP Montreal, and, of course, the headquarters—Los Angeles—Against The Stream Buddhist Meditation Society.

Big Love to all living beings!